# JONAH

## Navigating a Life Interrupted

# PRISCILLA SHIRER

LifeWay Press®. Nashville, Tennessee

Published by LifeWay Press®
© 2010 • Priscilla Shirer
Fifth printing 2012

ISBN 978-1-4158-6849-2
Item 005264295

Dewey Decimal classification: 224.02
Subject headings:  BIBLE. O.T. JONAH—STUDY \ GOD \ WILL \ JONAH, PROPHET

To order additional copies of this resource: Write LifeWay Church Resources Customer Service; One LifeWay Plaza; Nashville, TN 37234-0113; fax order to (615) 251-5933; phone (800) 458-2772; order online at www.lifeway.com; e-mail ordereentry@lifeway.com; or visit the LifeWay Christian Store serving you.

Printed in the United States of America

Leadership and Adult Publishing
LifeWay Church Resources
One LifeWay Plaza
Nashville, TN 37234-0175

# CONTENTS

# ABOUT THE AUTHOR

**PRISCILLA SHIRER** is a Bible teacher whose ministry is focused on the expository teaching of the Word of God to women. Her desire is to see women not only know the uncompromising truths of Scripture intellectually but also experience them practically by the power of the Holy Spirit. Priscilla is a graduate of Dallas Theological Seminary with a Master's degree in Biblical Studies. For over a decade she has been a conference speaker for major corporations, organizations, and Christian audiences across the United States and the world.

Priscilla is now in full-time ministry to women. She is the author of a handful of books and Bible studies including *A Jewel in His Crown*, *And We Are Changed*, *He Speaks to Me*, *Discerning the Voice of God*, and *One in a Million*.

Priscilla is the daughter of pastor, speaker, and well-known author Dr. Tony Evans. She is married to her best friend Jerry and spends her days cleaning up after three fabulous boys: Jackson, Jerry Jr., and Jude. Jerry and Priscilla have founded Going Beyond Ministries, where they are committed to seeing believers receive the most out of their relationships with the Lord.

# A Note From Priscilla

Interrupted lives—probably an accurate descriptor for all of us, don't you think? Whether with deliberate detail or inadvertent spontaneity, we each chart out a tidy yellow-brick road of goals for our lives. I certainly have. Without even realizing it, I've taken my life by the helm and asked God to conform to my flimsy timetable and arrangements.

This was never more clear than when baby Jude, our third spectacular gift from God, began growing in my tummy. We were shocked and a bit overwhelmed at the prospect of life with a newborn ... again. Yet through this new adventure, God began to expose my tendency to cling to my own plans instead of embracing His purposes for me, even when they differ from what I deem suited for my capabilities.

Your interruptions may differ from mine. In fact, I suspect they are. Life's too individual and unexpected to treat us all the same. Yet interruptions can be difficult to manage, no matter what—or whose—they are.

• looming retirement with a diminishing nest egg in a crumbling economy
• another year of singleness when you long for marriage
• a spouse's secret revealed that threatens your security
• a heartbreaking encounter with yet another year of battling infertility
• a burst of success in business that seems far beyond your capacity to manage
• redirection into ministry that means abandoning a lucrative corporate career
• a new baby (or two), requiring all the attention these little ones always do

Interruptions. They come in all sizes and shapes. All colors and shades. Good and bad. Though we wish to avoid them, every season of life seems to include a few—sometimes on either end of the same day. As we're coming up for air from the devastation of one, a fresh and exciting interruption takes our breath away, challenging us with new responsibilities, leaving us feeling inadequate and outmatched. They shock us; they shake us; they compel us to change. Sometimes they make us wonder if God even cares.

So, welcome to Jonah. He knows how a life interrupted feels, and he's got a firsthand account of how yielding to God is the best decision after all.

Join me, won't you?

Somehow, you know I had to say it, I think we'll have a "whale" of a time.

*Priscilla Shirer*

*" 'For My thoughts are not your thoughts,*
*nor are your ways My ways,' declares the LORD" (Isa. 55:8).*

How has your life been interrupted lately?

Every chapter, every verse in Jonah is about
the __grandeur__ of our God.

Jonah was the only prophet who received instructions from
God and __Ran__ from what God told him to do.

Our journey with Jonah helps us __Revamp__ our view
of life interrupted.

*"The word of the LORD came to Jonah the son of Amittai saying" (Jonah 1:1).*

THE __interrupted__ LIFE is the __privileged__ life.

The first two miracles in the Book of Jonah are found in the
very first verse.

1. God spoke.
2. God allowed a mere human to hear His voice.

To get a new view on what the interrupted life really means for
believers in Jesus Christ, we need to get a new view of God.

The _one true_ God comes down to talk to us.

When the interrupted life comes, say "I got it" and mean it.

*"Arise, go to Nineveh the great city and cry against it,*
*for their wickedness has come up before Me" (Jonah 1:2).*

One of the greatest revivals in history occurred because one man responded in obedience.

Jonah was a prophet. His job was to _hear_ the word of God and then to _Administer_ it to other people.

Nineveh was a place of hopelessness.

God often sends us into the _hopeless_ place because it's in the hopeless place that we can see the _hope_ of God.

## THE INTERRUPTED LIFE is the _significant_ life.

Second Kings 14:25 tells us five things about Jonah:

1. his name
2. his religion
3. his family
4. his job
5. his hometown

## THE INTERRUPTED LIFE is the cure for the _search_ for significance.

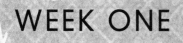

# I AM JONAH

# I AM JONAH

*"The word of the LORD came to Jonah the*
*son of Amittai saying." Jonah 1:1*

I am Jonah.
I want to serve God …
    as long as it is convenient.
I desire to do His will …
    until it is a tad uncomfortable.
I want to hear His Word …
    as long as its message is one I'm supposed
    to pass on to someone else.
I don't want to have my plans interrupted.
Oh yes. I am Jonah, and I suspect that in
    one way or another, you are too.

The story of Jonah has been a tale too extravagant and too outlandish for many people to believe as truth. They can't wrap their minds around the storm, the big fish, the city's revival, the sun, the east wind, and the plant that all play a role in this compelling narrative.

Were it not for my own firm belief in the inerrancy and validity of Scripture, I might doubt its veracity as well. Yet with all its unique qualities, I am drawn to the prophet and his true-life saga for one critical reason: Jonah was the only prophet who ever ran from God. I can relate to that. When my life and plans have been interrupted, I've wanted to rebel against it.

Have your life plans ever been interrupted?
☑ yes ○ no ○ not sure

Have you ever run from God? ☑ yes ○ no ○ not sure
Write your thoughts. *I have made career choices that God probably didn't want me to make*

If you answered yes to either of these questions, Jonah's story is your story.

# I hate to be interrupted!
## Say it with me now:
## "I HATE TO BE INTERRUPTED."

Yesterday I had a chance to relax for two hours. It was a delightful surprise to come across some quiet moments alone. I don't know how it happened, but Jerry ended up out of the house with all three of our little boys.

Yes, Lord!

Those two hours became precious to me. I became intent on guarding them. Anything that might invade my treasured plan to relax was overlooked to the best of my abilities. I didn't want to be disturbed.

You know the feeling, don't you? The disgust and overwhelming frustration that washes over you when you are derailed off your chosen course for your day or even the one free hour you surprisingly come across. If you do, then you can also imagine the compounded frustration of having a life that's been interrupted. We planned one thing for our lives, and yet our current situation looks nothing like what we had in mind. Someone tampered with our ambitions, goals, and dreams. The yellow-brick road of our lives veered off in some unexpected direction.

**What are some of your life goals that you've yet to see become a reality?**

*financial security*
*a lasting marriage*
*children*

**How has life tampered with those goals?**

*infertility*
*lack of financial security to persue adoption*
*marriage to someone who really didnt want kids*

Some changes we're delighted with. Others disappoint us and leave us buried in questions. Without a firm belief in the goodness and the care of God, we can spend years mad at ourselves, mad at others, or even mad at Him because we didn't get to accomplish what we originally set out to do.

**In the margin list three adjectives that describe how you feel about interruptions you've faced in your life plans.**

*Sad, frustrated, disappointed*

Often we equate the term *interruption* with upheaval, derailing, and frustration. Who wouldn't try to avoid those? Yet a closer look reveals an issue of value. When we deem our current task as an essential priority, we'll look with contempt on anything that threatens our time focused on it. Why? We've given priority and credited value to the current task, person, or goal.

We learn about Jonah's priorities in 2 Kings 14:25, the only other time he is mentioned in the Old Testament.

**According to 2 Kings 14:25, what was Jonah's job?**

*A prophet*

**Was he successful at his job, and how did you determine your answer?**

*yes, because Israel's boundaries were restored as Jonah prophesied*

As a prophet to the Northern Kingdom of Israel, Jonah's priorities would have included:
1. hearing from God
2. declaring God's messages to His people
3. being identified as a true prophet of God

I believe God and His will held prominent importance to Jonah. He loved his people and wanted to see them rise in power and influence. It seems Jonah likely enjoyed success because what he prophesied was happening.

**From your personal goals you wrote, would you say you gave highest importance to God and His will?**

*No*

During the reign of King Jeroboam II, the nation's territories that had been taken by Syria were restored. While we know little of Jonah's life prior to the events in the chapters we're studying, we do know he had foretold these good things for his people. As a result he most likely was popular, highly respected, and appreciated. In addition, he probably enjoyed financial security.

**Read Jonah 1:3. What might this verse reveal about Jonah's financial security?**

*He was financially secure enough to pay fare on a ship*

Jonah lived in a time of national economic prosperity. Israel regained lost territories and achieved its most prosperous time since Solomon. Israel's wealth exploded because it controlled important trade routes

*"[King Jeroboam] restored the border of Israel from the entrance of Hamath as far as the Sea of the Arabah, according to the word of the LORD, the God of Israel, which He spoke through His servant Jonah the son of Amittai, the prophet who was of Gath-hepher."*
**2 Kings 14:25**

through Palestine that connected the ancient world. In fact, some rabbinic commentators think the Hebrew text implies Jonah chartered the entire ship, cargo and all.[1] If so, he must have had adequate financial means.

According to Jonah 1:1, Jonah's interruption began when "The word of the LORD came" to him. His priorities and life of comfort were disrupted with directives that would put him in an entirely new and different direction than that which he was currently enjoying.

> **What do you think might have been some of the comforts Jonah had to leave behind in Israel to follow God's instructions?**

*Home/shelter*
*Security*

> **If your life is being interrupted right now in some way, what "comforts" are you having the most difficult time leaving behind to follow God's directives?**

*Lack of Relationship/children*
*Lack of financial security*

## CHANGING PERSPECTIVE

I wish Jonah could have seen his life laid out in four simple chapters like we can. He would have seen that what he considered an interruption was really an invitation to participate in one of the more supernatural events in all the Old Testament—one that would not only make a mark in the Old but the New Testament as well (Luke 11:30). He couldn't have known that his story would be studied by millions desiring to draw closer to his God.

Yet Jonah probably felt about God's plans the same way you and I often feel—he was frustrated. The importance and priority we've placed on our plans cause us to frown on new assignments the Lord may send our way.

> **What other challenges might you face that will make it difficult for you to see life interruptions in a positive way?**

Our study of Jonah is primarily about helping us to redefine interruption when it comes to our relationship with God. If He is our priority and His will is our primary purpose, then when the "word of the LORD" comes to us or when He allows us to see His hand in our circumstances, we must see it as an esteemed opportunity to participate in kingdom purposes. What more critical or essential ambition could there be?

So today, my friend, right at the onset of our study, we redefine interruption. God's plan is a "Divine Intervention."

### Consider the following equation:

Insignificant Person + Insignificant Task = Interruption

Significant Person + Significant Task = Divine Intervention

### Explain the meaning of the equation in your own words.

*If we attach meaning to the task (regard it as a priority) it has a purpose*

> If you find yourself balking at God's instructions in your life, it is an indication of the importance you place on God and His will.

Interruptions only become positive when we consider the person or the circumstance interrupting to be more significant than that which currently occupies our attention. It is easy to say that God and His plans are our most essential endeavors. It is entirely another thing to live like this is so.

While I love a good in-depth study with deep exploratory questions, I was continually drawn to ask you personal application questions while writing this study. When you turn the last page, you'll no doubt know more about Jonah's story than you may have before, but my primary goal in our time together is to help you dig deeply into its application to your life. Many of the questions I will ask you will focus on how Jonah's story relates to you.

Reworking our view of God and His plans is our goal, particularly this first week. To handle life's interruptions appropriately, the prophet needed a fresh view of God, and over the course of the next few days of his life that is exactly what he was going to get. My prayer is that these seven weeks we spend together will do the same for you and me.

As we place God and His will in a position of significance, I pray that we will be delighted when we hear His voice or see His hand orchestrating our circumstances to align with His purposes.

Conclude today's lesson by listing in the margin your top three aspirations at this point in your life. It could be a goal you have for your children, your career, ministry, finances, or something else. Then take time to meditate on whether you place more importance on them or on God and His purposes for you. Will you yield them to Him if He requests that you do so?

*Financial security*
*Relationship*
*Discovering God's purpose for my life*

# ON THE JOB

*"For we are God's fellow workers." 1 Corinthians 3:9*

I recently met a young woman who works as a personal assistant to one of the most powerful people in the country. She was delighted when she was offered this coveted job working alongside this highly respected and busy individual. The moment she signed on to be an assistant, she was told that during her working hours she needed to be on call. This meant that at any moment her boss may call her to assist him and she would need to drop anything she was doing—even if she were working on another assignment at the time. While adjusting to fit this schedule was difficult at first, she quickly became used to it and organized her life appropriately.

Now she is constantly waiting on a call from her boss. She makes sure that all of her communication devices are powered up, activated, and just a hand's reach away so that she can be ready to receive instruction. While she does make some personal plans during working hours, she holds them loosely. She is fully aware that her primary responsibility is to be ready to manage that which her boss assigns.

I asked her if she felt overwhelmed or disgusted having to change her personal plans. She shook her head and replied, "No way. It's an honor to have this job. And," she added, "he's a nice guy. While everything he asks for is not always convenient, he's very considerate. I want to do a good job."

*"The LORD is righteous in all His ways and kind in all His deeds."*
**Psalm 145:17**

When we signed up to follow Christ, we automatically signed up to be open to "Divine Intervention"—God interruptions. While His "call" might not always be convenient or easy, responding to it should not just be a duty but our joy. We are getting the honor of partnering with the Lord in His purposes for this generation. You can count on the promise in Psalm 145:17. He is kind in all of His ways so you don't have to worry that He may take advantage of your loyalty. Partnering with Him doesn't mean having no plans and ambitions of your own. It means holding them loosely, always leaving room for "the word of the LORD" reshaping your purposes and aligning them with His own.

**Rewrite our equations from yesterday's lesson.**

Jonah had been a prophet to Israel; now he was being called to Nineveh. (See Jonah 1:2.) Take a moment to find this location on the map in the back of your book and circle it.

**Based on Jonah's response, did he consider this a divine intervention or an interruption? Explain.**

*An interruption – he hopped a ship going in the opposite direction of Nineveh*

**In the chart below, write how the biblical character was interrupted. Did he see God's instruction as a divine intervention or a negative interruption? Explain.**

| Name | God's Directive | Interruption or Divine Intervention |
|------|-----------------|-------------------------------------|
| Noah | Genesis 6:13-14,17-22 | *Divine intervention – He did as he was told* |
| Gideon | Judges 6:11-27 | *Divine intervention – He doubted his ability, but did as he was told* |
| Cornelius | Acts 10:1-8 | *Divine intervention, – he obeyed* |

In the first half of the 8th century B.C., Nineveh was one of the principal provinces in Assyria. The Assyrians had a reputation for inflicting physical and psychological terror on its enemies, including Israel. The Assyrians may have laid siege to Gath-hepher, Jonah's hometown. "Perhaps the city was destroyed and many of the inhabitants slain. Some loved one of Jonah may have suffered and been killed at this time. There is a possibility that his own mother and father were slain before his eyes when he was a boy."[2]

While we can only speculate about details of how Nineveh affected Jonah, Israel definitely had been brutalized by their archenemy. Just the name *Nineveh* would strike bitterness, dread, and fear in the heart of an Israelite. During the 8th century, Assyria was experiencing a time of national weakness and Jonah would have wanted to have seen their decline continue. It would have been his desire to see their complete demise. Yet God was calling Jonah to leave his beloved countrymen and preach to his enemies. Jonah placed no value on Nineveh or on its inhabitants.

I'll never forget a Rwandan couple coming forward for prayer in our church many years ago. They had been evacuated with other survivors during the vast murders of 1994. However, in the rush to leave the country, their children had been left behind. They didn't know if they were alive or dead and could only hope to see them again. The pain in that mother's eyes and the tears falling down the father's face is seared in my memory forever.

Many genocides have taken place in our lifetime. Hundreds of thousands of people have lost their lives at the hands of renegade governments, soldiers, or dictators. While most of us have not been directly affected by this, consider how you might feel if your family suffered at the hands of others and then you were asked to show mercy and concern for them.

**Did you grow up with a hatred or fear of any group of people? If so, in the margin note who and why.** no

God calling Jonah to Nineveh most likely struck the cord of a gut-level, deep-seated hurt with just the mention of the city's name. He had an enormous dislike for this place and its inhabitants.

In our journeys with God, we will likely come across our personal Ninevehs. For some this might actually be a place; for others Nineveh is a task or relationship and just the mention of that mission or person sends us into an emotional tailspin. We'd just rather not go. And, like Jonah, we can point to many reasons that would keep us at home.

**Do you have a Nineveh assignment—something God is requiring of you right now that you do not want to do? What are your reasons for not wanting to do it?**
I don't know what I'm supposed to be doing

### MISSIONARY ASSIGNMENT

During the video lesson I encouraged you to start considering how your group can tangibly and practically minister to others during the course of your study. Begin to consider who the Ninevites may be in your world—the unloved, forgotten, seemingly unreachable ones.

## PRIVILEGED TO BE INTERRUPTED

God graciously gives divine interventions to His children. He presents them an opportunity to partner with Him in purposes they could never conceive. A life interrupted by a holy God is a privilege. Believers must internalize this principle in order to live a life that accomplishes God's will.

God doesn't need us to complete His purposes, yet He still chooses to ask us to partner with Him. It's unfathomable. His calling you means that He has chosen you above anyone else to do what He is asking. You are the one He singled out and pinpointed as His partner for a particular project.

Whether it's parenting a special needs child, starting a Bible study, remaining single for a bit longer, or even, like Jonah, reaching out to those who hurt you, He's purposefully given you the high honor of being the one He deemed suited for a task that has heavenly implications—a task of divine partnership that will yield magnificent results for you and for His kingdom. While these benefits might not be visible at the outset, a supernatural outcome waits on the horizon for anyone who chooses to partner with God.

> God's calling you means He has chosen you above anyone else.

**For each of the biblical characters you just studied, how did each culminate in unimaginable results?**

Noah (Gen. 8:18-22) – *God vowed never again to destroy all living creatures*

Gideon (Judg. 8:22) – *Gideon was asked to rule over the Israelites because he saved them from the Midianites*

Cornelius (Acts 10:30-48) – *Because Peter was brought to Cornelius' home as God asked, all who heard his word were baptized & received the Holy Spirit*

**From the following verses, list the ways Jonah's life became one of eternal significance:**

Jonah 3:4-5 *Because the Ninevites listened to Jonahs' words & repented they were spared*

Luke 11:30 *– As Jonah was a sign to Ninevites, Jesus was a sign in his generation. All Ninevites would stand at judgement time because they repented*

Believing that divine interruptions are a privilege not only will cause us to handle them differently but also to await them eagerly. Knowing that we have an opportunity to participate in God's purposes should cause us to sit on the edge of our seats in anticipation of divine interventions disguised as life's interruptions.

## SIGNIFICANTLY YOU

We know very little about Jonah. In fact, until the four chapters of this book, his life seems fairly insignificant. Jonah is a lone character with one known relative: his father. His dad's name and his birthplace are only mentioned twice in the entirety of Scripture. No other record of his lineage

"[King Jeroboam] restored the border of Israel from the entrance of Hamath as far as the Sea of the Arabah, according to the word of the LORD, the God of Israel, which He spoke through His servant Jonah the son of Amittai, the prophet, who was of Gath-hepher."
2 Kings 14:25

exists. Everything we know about the prophet before the Book of Jonah shows up in 2 Kings 14:25. Pay special attention to it now.

**Record Jonah's "résumé" from 2 Kings.**

**His name:** Jonah

**His hometown:** Gath-hepher

**His religion:** Christian

**His job:** prophet

**His closest relative:** father (Amittai)

These five details about Jonah sum up what we know about him. Nothing is particularly noteworthy. Not until he received a divine interruption did he develop a life story that made a stamp on history. The bulk of what Scripture teaches about this prophet and certainly the most eternally significant part of this man's life comes after God interrupted.

When Jonah heard a word from God—and finally yielded to it—his ordinary existence became extraordinary. Not only did Jonah spark the greatest revival in all human history but as a result of his mission he was mentioned in the New Testament by Jesus. Jonah's true significance began with a divine intervention.

## Divine Intervention + Yielded Submission = ETERNAL SIGNIFICANCE

**Rewrite this equation in your own words below.**

When we yield to God's call (interruption) willingly, long lasting results occur

When God chose Jonah to go to Nineveh, it was a privilege. His story began when he yielded to God's divine intervention, and it made an eternal imprint on humanity. Whatever God has called you to do should be a privilege for you to undertake. While it might not be easy or convenient, He offers you a chance to write a story of significance for eternity.

# MAKE YOUR MARK

*"Whatever things were gain to me, those things I have counted as loss for the sake of Christ." Philippians 3:7*

Last fall I got a chance to participate in a wonderful event. It was for young people who were just starting out in positions of leadership in ministry. The theme of the event was "Make Your Mark." In different workshops and sessions they were being encouraged to stay open to God's leading in their ministries as they could only leave a lasting imprint to the extent that they chose to yield to and follow God.

Most biblical people who made a lasting mark in Christianity had a point in their lives where they stood at a crossroad. They had to decide to yield to divine intervention at the cost of their own plans or continue on their own path instead. From Noah's call to build an unfamiliar object called an ark to Peter being told to go to the house of a Gentile named Cornelius, any person God used mightily for His glory both began and continued his or her journey with divine interruptions. As they yielded to God's purposes, they unknowingly wrote life stories that made a mark on humanity.

**Yesterday you listed the five facts we learned about Jonah from 2 Kings 14:25. Record these same facts about yourself.**

Name:

Hometown:

Denomination:

Job:

Closest relative:

I want to admit to you that in younger years, my significance was wrapped up in some of these facts. As a daughter of a prominent minister, I have a wonderful legacy of family and faith. Yet the story God is writing in my life and the mark that He wants me to make cannot be based on my family, the legacy of faith they may leave, or the work they have done for His sake. My mark must be mine—orchestrated by God and separate from the great and admirable work He has done in the lives of those I love.

*My job, but I never felt successful or accomplished at anything*

**Look back at your "résumé." Put a check mark beside any in which you have tried to seek your significance. In the margin, explain and plan to discuss with your group.**

Trouble for believers always comes when they try to stake their claim to significance, even unknowingly, with any of these five things. If who you are, where you are from, what church you go to, what you do for a living, or who you are related to or associated with becomes the thing you hang your hat of significance on, you will eventually find yourself wanting. Our significance, at least the kind that will leave an eternal mark, can only really be found in how fully we yield to God's purposes for our lives.

Possibly you are on the other side of the spectrum. Maybe the places or people you are associated with do not make you proud. Maybe you've not achieved nearly as much as you would have liked or, like me, your past is cluttered with the remnants of a slew of consequences from bad choices you've made. Maybe, like Jonah, you don't have a rich family legacy to speak of or major accomplishments to highlight and you feel that God could not possibly want to use you to achieve something extraordinary. On the contrary, Scripture is replete with stories of men and women who were used mightily of God despite how their résumé reads.

**Choose two of the following characters who most interest you or whom you know the least about. Read the references; then record your answers in the margin.**

**ESTHER**

*Raised by cousin Mordechai after her parents died.*

What was her life like (Esth. 2:5-7)?

*She was brought to the palace & chosen by King Xerxes to be queen*

How did divine intervention change that (Esth. 2:8-9,17-18)?

*Petitioned the King to spare her people*

How did she make her mark (Esth. 4:14-16; 7:1-4; 8:11-14)?

**MARY**

*Lived in Nazareth, Engaged to Joseph*

What was her life like (Luke 1:26-27)?

*She was chosen to give birth to Jesus*

How did divine intervention change that (Luke 1:30-35)?

*She did as she was called to do and gave birth to the Savior*

How did she make her mark (Luke 2:7)?

**RAHAB**

What was her life like (Josh. 2:1)?

How did divine intervention change that (Josh. 2:2-6)?

How did she make her mark (Heb. 11:31; Matt. 1:5)?

PETER
What was his life like (Matt 4:18)?
How did divine intervention change that (Matt. 4:19)?
How did he make his mark (Matt. 16:18)?

What other biblical characters come to mind who had similar experiences?

# DECLARATION OF DEPENDENCE

What most of us really want is autonomy. We'd like to have independence and freedom to govern our own path. We want to make a mark but only on our terms. We don't mind following Christ as long as His path eventually converges onto the one we already had chosen. We want to select our own course, run after our own ambitions, and decide how to make use of our own time. So when anyone—including God—steps in and makes demands that interrupt our goals, we push back.

Single women rebel against singleness when it's gone on longer than they expected. Mothers get frustrated at the demands of caring for a family when they anticipated conquering corporate America. Ministers want to give up when God's way for them means teaching 20 faithful folks every week instead of stadiums full. Leaders want to throw in the towel when their mission meets with resistance that threatens to give them a harder time than they expected. Interruptions have a way of revealing whether we really mean it when we say, "Lord, not my will but Yours be done." Today is as good a day as any to write a declaration of our dependence on God.

Pause. Take a moment to let the Lord reveal your heart. Be honest with Him about where you are in relation to your declaration of dependence.

We have the benefit of reading the ending of the stories of Bible characters. We skip ahead and find the outcome they did not have the luxury of knowing at the time. They may not have realized the privilege and certainly didn't know the eternal impact they would make. How could they have known that their names would go down in God's Word to encourage us millennia later? At the time they chose to yield to their divine intervention, it was completely by faith in God.

Like these holy heroes, you've got an outcome you can't make out. The fog of life's journey will clog your spiritual sight, and the fear of the unknown is bound to make you consider bowing out. Don't back down. In future generations, your story will be the one that encourages someone else to follow hard after God. Have you ever considered that just as the previous stories encourage us along the way, yours will encourage someone else?

Make sure your life writes a story worth reading. Correctly viewing and appreciating God's awesomeness and His love compel you to realize the distinct privilege of being used by Him.

Your story starts with God. The mark you make and your eternal significance will be found in yielding to the divine intervention God sends your way. When the Lord speaks over your life, separating you unto Himself for His purposes or allowing circumstances to derail you from your original plan, consider it your invitation. You've been given the opportunity to write a story beyond your expectations. Beginning in chapter 1, Jonah's tale unfolds and immediately he becomes more than just a résumé from 2 Kings. He becomes a significant part of God's purposes for entire nations of people.

Your story begins with God's call. It is not your legacy or lack thereof that makes you significant. It is God's call and your willingness to obey it.

> God's call and your willingness to obey make you significant.

**You previously detailed Bible characters who became significant through divine interruption. Now it's your turn. Detail how you've seen life interruptions offer you an invitation to eternal significance.**

**Your name:**

**What was your life like?**

*In a rut in California*

**How has divine intervention already changed that?**

*I believe God brought me to Maine, but I don't know why.*

**How are you significant as a result?**

*I still don't know*

End today by doing two things. First, prepare to share your story of divine intervention. Consider how God might be preparing each person to leave a mark on humanity. Second, use the margin to write your own declaration of dependence. You only need a few strong sentences to state your intention to turn away from autonomous living and to full faith in Him.

*Lord help me to discover your purpose for my life so I can step into the fullness of that destiny.*

Day 4

# THE REAL STAR

*"We all, with unveiled faces, are reflecting the glory of the Lord and are being transformed into the same image from glory to glory; this is from the Lord who is the Spirit." 2 Corinthians 3:18*

"Dream Girls" was a breakout hit a few years ago. Theaters were filled with moviegoers riveted by this musical on the big screen. Beyonce Knowles was set up to be the breakout star of the film but the "sleeper" in the movie surprised and awed viewers. Jennifer Hudson garnered an Academy Award for her portrayal of Effie. Her acting chops and moving vocals catapulted her into celebrity status. She became the real star.

On first glance, the principal character in the book we're studying appears to be Jonah, but a closer look reveals that the title character in this narrative is God Himself. If you keep your attention keen and your eyes peeled in these four short chapters, you'll be overwhelmed and awed to discover Him all over again. His attributes, His character, and His ability swim through the entire book and therefore Jonah's life.

The story opens with the word of the Lord (1:1), centers around the acts of the Lord, and concludes with the word of the Lord (4:9-11). From beginning to end, it's all about Him. Beyond any doubt, the main character is God. It's a good thing since having a fresh view of Him is paramount if we are to begin believing that life interruptions are really divine interventions.

> We've become so enamored with the big fish, we've lost sight of a big God.

From day 1, fill in the blanks.

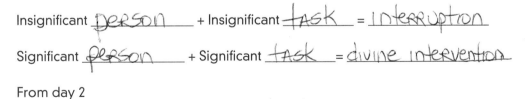

Insignificant <u>person</u> + Insignificant <s>task</s> = <u>interruption</u>

Significant <u>person</u> + Significant <s>task</s> = <u>divine intervention</u>

From day 2

Divine Interruption + Yielded <u>submission</u> = Eternal <u>significance</u>

Making an eternal mark on earth should be our most important goal because God is not only the headliner of Jonah's story but He's also the title character of yours as well. As long as you view Him as insignificant, you'll think His plans for you are too. The result will be continual frustration as you run from or ignore His attempts to guide you toward His best for you. His best includes predetermined purposes that you've been specifically equipped to master.

Giving God a position of significance—the primary role—in your daily living is of paramount importance. This means more than simply receiving Him as Savior. In the tale of your life unfolding right now, He, not you, must be the One in the spotlight. Your life involves you but is not ultimately about you. Knowing this allows you to be more willing to relinquish control over your life and yield to the divine intervention.

> Your life involves you but is not ultimately about you.

## OWNERSHIP VS. MANAGEMENT

Jonah is a quintessential picture of a person who serves God and yet still seeks to hold the title role in his story. He'd been given the gift of prophecy and was willing to use it as long as he could do it in the place and among the people he desired. As soon as God's will led Jonah outside of that comfort zone, he opted out. Jonah had done what we often do—take ownership of that which we've only been asked to manage.

Note that God didn't change what He wanted Jonah to do. Jonah was still called to declare God's message. God just altered where and to whom Jonah was to do it. When God asserted His role as owner of the gift He'd given Jonah, the prophet couldn't take it. The same often happens to us as well. We receive a gift from God—a call to ministry or spiritual gift to edify His body—and subconsciously take ownership of it. We become disgruntled when God tells us to use it in a way we hadn't planned.

**How would you describe the difference between being an owner and a manager?**

*A manager merely oversees that which is owned by someone else*

**What type of giftings has God given you?** = *gift of salvation*
*- I don't see them (as far as talents)*
*- I've been blessed with good health & a roof over my head*

**Has He ever asked you to utilize them in a way you didn't anticipate? If so, did you handle His request as if you were the owner or manager? Describe.**

How might usurping God's role as owner complicate one's life? *Trying to take charge rather than letting God have control, can delay his plans for us*

I read a story about a king who sent a message to the ruler of an enemy kingdom. The messenger, hoping the king was declaring war on the enemy, decided to read the letter. He was appalled to discover his king was offering a peace treaty. He decided to take matters into his own hands. He'd simply bury it and craft a lie to tell when he got back home.

His plan was interrupted when scouts from the enemy kingdom discovered him burying the letter, seized him and the note, and delivered them to the king. Peace was established and the messenger released, but he was disappointed and disillusioned at what his king had allowed.

The courier had made a major error. He put himself in the position of owner when he was only supposed to be a manager.

Have you taken ownership of any areas of your life that you should be managing for the King? If so, list one.
*Trusting God completely with my finances*

How has this affected your life?
*Causes worry & stress*

How might your life be different if you switch roles from owner to manager?
*More peace*

## THE PRINCIPLE OF PURPOSE

The apostle Paul helped us remember the difference between ownership and management by teaching us the principle of purpose.

Rewrite Ephesians 2:10 in your own words.
*We are created by God to fulfill His destiny for our lives*

25

The message can never be underscored enough for the believer in Christ. Look at the progression of the principles the verse teaches:

1. You are His.
2. You are His workmanship.
3. You are a masterpiece recreated in Christ Jesus.
4. You are created masterfully for the purpose of being equipped to accomplish good works.
5. You are equipped to accomplish good works that were prepared beforehand by God.
6. You are equipped to accomplish preplanned good works by simply walking in them.

**Put the number of the portion of Ephesians 2:10 that is reinforced by each of the following passages and underline the key words from the verse that helped you make the connection.**

5  *Jeremiah 1:5, MSG*—"Before I shaped you in the womb, I knew all about you. Before you saw the light of day, I had holy plans for you: A prophet to the nations—that's what I had in mind for you."

5  *2 Timothy 2:21, NET*—"So if someone cleanses himself of such behavior, he will be a vessel for honorable use, set apart, useful for the Master, prepared for every good work."

3  *Ephesians 4:24, NLT*—"Put on your new nature, created to be like God—truly righteous and holy."

6  *1 John 2:6, NASB*—"The one who says he abides in Him ought himself to walk in the same manner as He walked."

2  *Psalm 139:14, NASB*—"I will give thanks to You, for I am fearfully and wonderfully made; Wonderful are Your works, and my soul knows it very well."

5  *2 Timothy 3:16-17, NASB* —"All Scripture is inspired by God and profitable for teaching, for reproof, for correction, for training in righteousness; so that the man of God may be adequate, equipped for every good work."

**John 17:9, NASB**—"'I ask on their behalf; I do not ask on behalf of the world, but of those whom You have given Me; for they are Yours.'"

*"O that My people would listen to Me. That Israel would walk in My ways!"*
**Psalm 81:13**

Recognizing and internalizing the Principle of Purpose is critical. Walking fully in God's plans for your life—that are intertwined with His purposes for humanity—hinges on whether you buy into the fact that you are His and have a purpose, a purpose you might not fully comprehend by using only human brain matter.

You were created with specific intention and recreated at the moment of your salvation with specific attention to detail so that you would be equipped to walk in the plans God mapped out for you long ago. You cannot reach complete satisfaction in life apart from your decision to engage in His predetermined plans. For Jonah and for us, this means giving Him the position of prominence in our lives and restructuring our plans so that we can partner with Him.

**Do any specific personal challenges make it difficult for you to embrace that God has a purpose for you?**

*financial struggles*

## THIS IS GOD'S STORY

Your life is God's story being told and His character being displayed. How does your life read? What is your life telling others about the God you serve? As a result of your decisions, do they get to see Him displayed in His best light?

Just as we can see God clearly through Jonah's story, God can and will be seen in ours. As we surrender to divine interventions (or not), each chapter of our lives puts God on display. We can see many characteristics of God in each chapter of Jonah. Here are a few of the highlights.

> **Jonah 1**—God is sovereign.
> **Jonah 2**—God is our Deliverer.
> **Jonah 3**—God is merciful.
> **Jonah 4**—God is righteous.

Today I want you to consider whether God has the title role in the story of your life. What words might you use to describe what this chapter of your life is declaring to others about God? In your current season and station, what do others learn about Him as they watch the way you live? Use the margin to record your thoughts.

# MAKING SENSE OF IT ALL

*"I have still many things to say to you, but you are not able to bear them or to take them upon you or to grasp them now." John 16:12, The Amplified Bible*

As we close our first week, I'll say what is probably on both our minds: Very little about the Book of Jonah makes sense. From a huge fish swallowing a man to an entire city turning from wickedness in 24 hours, the only way to account for the happenings in these chapters is to believe that God works miracles and that He has a plan that supersedes our senses.

From the onset, God's instructions didn't make sense to Jonah for many reasons. First, Jonah's ministry had been focused on foretelling the expansion and prosperity of Israel. Assyria was an enemy nation. If Nineveh received God's mercy, they might stand in the way of Israel's prosperity.

Second, scholars believed that going to Nineveh wouldn't have been a simple trip to make. Doing so would have meant Jonah selling all of his earthly possessions to which he might never return. He'd have to leave behind the comforts of economic security and the familiarity of his beloved country to venture into a pagan culture where he would be economically and politically weak. Why would God ask him to do this?

Third, Israel was God's covenant people. They were His chosen nation. The Ninevites were Gentiles. In Jonah's estimation, neither they nor any other group of people were supposed to be granted the mercy that had been extended to Israel. They were to be separate from all other people.

To Jonah, God's directions did not make sense.

**What doesn't seem to make sense about something God is asking of you right now?**

*— I don't know what God is asking of me - what He wants me to do career-wise*
*— I do believe He is asking me to become more active in sharing His word - I'm praying on both these things (how to do them)*

When you consider all the reasons why God's plans don't make sense, you might feel justified in running away. That kind of deception is typical of our hearts and minds.

Why be careful about following our feelings and wisdom according to Jeremiah 17:9 and Proverbs 28:26?

*Because they can deceive us & can't be trusted*

God's plans for us are so overwhelmingly beyond anything that we could ever imagine that our feelings or ability to reason His directives cannot be the determining factor for choosing obedience. Making sense of what God has asked or feeling compelled to cooperate cannot be the prerequisite for choosing obedience. His Word must be enough.

Study Judges 7:2-8,16. Why might God's instructions not have made sense to Gideon? How did he respond?

*It doesn't make sense that God was telling him he had too many men to fight, but Gideon obeyed.*

*"Lean on, trust in, and be confident in the Lord with all your heart and mind and do not rely on your own insight or understanding."*
**Proverbs 3:5, AMP**

## HYPOTHETICALLY SPEAKING

Picture a stunning encounter with God. You are alone in your home and have an experience that can only be described as being like Paul's experience while traveling to Damascus. You see a bright light and hear a voice that resonates with authority and power. You don't have any doubt who is speaking to you. You know it is God Himself. He gives you clear instructions to quit your high-paying job, immediately sell the house you just purchased last year and everything in it, pack up your family, and move to Kenya to minister to a primitive tribe that He will direct you to.

What would your next step be?
○ ignore the encounter with God
○ tell myself it couldn't be God since the directions were illogical and nonsensical
○ tell my spouse and hope he'd tell me that I was just imagining things
☑ seek wise counsel before moving forward — *pray about it*
○ (if I knew for sure it was God,) I'd put my house on the market immediately.

While this is an extreme illustration, we see our natural tendencies most clearly against the backdrop of intense situations. How you responded to the above hypothetical situation may reveal how you respond when God's divine interruption requires only slight lifestyle modifications.

> **What is the last thing you felt compelled by God's Spirit to do? Was your response similar to or completely different than your selection above? In what way?**
>
> *Move to Maine – my response was similar since I prayed about it.*

## THE MYSTERY OF HIS WILL

**Missionary Assignment**

List some reasons why you think God's modern day people have forgotten His heart for others. How can your group combat this?

When the Book of Jonah was written, its original purpose was to be read to the Israelites. God desired that Jonah's mission remind the nation of something that wouldn't have made sense to them. God had a heart for others outside of Israel and wanted to dispense His mercy to them as well. This principle from Jonah's story lays the framework for a message that the apostle Paul continued to convince the Jews of centuries later.

> **Read Ephesians 3:2-4,6. What did Paul tell the believers in Ephesus was "the great mystery"?**
>
> *Through the gospel, Gentiles & Israelites are both heirs & share God's promise through Christ*

As the prosperity and security of Israel increased, the idea of God's family including their enemies would not have seemed logical. And yet, despite their ability to comprehend God's desires, they were being compelled to respond accordingly.

> **Fill in the blanks in Jonah 2:9 below.**
> **"But I will sacrifice to You with the voice of thanksgiving. That which I have** *Vowed* **I will pay.** *Salvation* **is from** *the Lord* **."**

Many commentators believe that the message of the Book of Jonah to Israel hinges on this verse. As Jonah soaked in the gastric fluids and rotting foods in the fish's belly, he most likely drifted in and out of consciousness. In those moments, I believe he realized how much trouble following his good senses had gotten him into. Now he recognized that "salvation," which means continued deliverance and sure victory, can only come to those who are yielded to God. Those yielded to Him, even when the directives don't make sense and even when difficulty is encountered, rest in the knowledge that they are safeguarded by Him.

Engaging in God's will is not always comfortable or convenient, but it is worth it. The yielded ones are guaranteed the benefits that only come to those who have chosen to camp out in His hedge of protection.

**Rewrite the meaning of this equation.**
**Divine Intervention + Yielded Submission = Salvation**
**from the Lord**

> Salvation comes to those who yield to God's will

**In light of today's theme, personalize and rewrite the truth found in Luke 11:28.**

> Those who hear & obey the word of God are blessed.

Close your lesson by noting in the margin the parts of your journey with God right now that don't make sense to you. Then talk to the Lord honestly. Thank Him for the divine intervention that is your invitation to partner with Him. Meditate on what it will mean to engage fully in His calling even if it is shrouded in the mystery of His eternal will. If you are ready, make a commitment to yield to Him and His purposes even when they don't make sense.

## Navigation Tools

At the end of each week's study, take a moment to record the principles that most impacted you and can help you to navigate your journey through the interrupted life. Note this week's navigation tools:

**Day 1** We should look on interruptions as divine interventions

**Day 2** Interventions are an opportunity to leave an eternal imprint

**Day 3** Your willingness to obey God's call makes you significant

**Day 4** God is in charge — has ownership

**Day 5** Are we willing to follow God's call?

# Session 2
## VIEWER GUIDE

THE INTERRUPTED LIFE is the _Challenging_ life.

*It's hard to do what God wants when we're comfortable where we're at. We don't want to "Arise & go" do what God wants at that time.*

*"Arise, go to Nineveh the great city and cry against it, for their wickedness has come up before Me" (Jonah 1:2).*

God will give you _Strength_ to handle the challenge.

The Holy Spirit is the Third Person of the Trinity revealed to us in Scripture.

If you are a believer of Jesus Christ, all of the _power_, _greatness_, grandeur, _Authority_ and fullness of God Himself is in you because the Holy Spirit is on the inside of you.

※ [ Oftentimes the greatest hindrance of a new move of God in your life is the last move of God. *(We're comfortable with the last thing He did*)

God loves to put us in the challenge because that's where He gets to be _who_ _He_ _is_.

We let our feelings, our "want to," talk us out of obeying God. *we don't obey because we don't want to*

*"Delight yourself in the LORD; and He will give you the desires of your heart" (Ps. 37:4).* *He will Align your desires w/ His desires if you are obedient*

*"Incline my heart to Your testimonies and not to dishonest gain. Turn away my eyes from looking at vanity, and revive me in Your ways" (Ps. 119:36-37).*

THE INTERRUPTED LIFE not only looks _different_ but also looks more _difficult_ .

When God places an _Abnormal_ calling on your life, it is because He has abnormal _results_ He wants to produce through you. (supernatural)

THE INTERRUPTED LIFE is the _Accountable_ life. — God requires a response to His call

*"But Jonah rose up to flee to Tarshish from the presence of the LORD. So he went down to Joppa, found a ship which was going to Tarshish, paid the fare and went down into it to go with them to Tarshish from the presence of the LORD"* (Jonah 1:3).

God does not _Convict_ us to _Condemn_ us. He wants to _Restore_ relationship.

Sin is a never-ending downward spiral, a never-ending downward cycle.

God is waiting to rescue you!

# SEE JONAH RUN

Day 1

# ON THE RUN

*"But Jonah rose up to flee to Tarshish from the presence of the LORD. So he went down to Joppa, found a ship which was going to Tarshish, paid the fare and went down into it to go with them to Tarshish from the presence of the LORD." Jonah 1:3*

White House/Black Market. It's a great women's clothing store ... if you like black and white. The first time I stepped into this boutique I walked through a sea of black and white pants, tops, skirts, and jewelry, stopped suddenly in shock and whispered, "These people really only sell things that are black or white?"

Duh. Shouldn't have taken me that long to figure it out.

For the patron interested in colorful options, this retailer is not for you. Coming into this store limits you to two alternatives. It's that simple. It's black and white.

There's no gray area in obeying God either, you know. When God speaks or allows you to see His hand, giving you the opportunity to participate in His purposes, you don't have an array of options to choose from on how you will respond. It's clear-cut, plain and simple ... black and white. You can either choose to obey or choose to disobey. No neutral ground. Choosing to "do nothing" is really a decision to delay obedience—and the word for delayed obedience? Disobedience.

**Read Jonah 1:1-3 and answer the following questions:**

**Where did God tell Jonah to go?** Nineveh

**Where did Jonah go?** Joppa (To hop a ship to Tarshish)

**Locate Joppa and Tarshish on the map in the back of your book and mark their locations with an "x."**

After clearly hearing God's direction, Jonah ran to the nearest seaport at Joppa to find a ship bound for Tarshish. While its exact location is unknown, Tarshish was a Phoenician colony, probably at the southern tip of Spain—in the opposite direction of Nineveh. Nineveh was 500 miles to the east while Tarshish was 2,000 miles west. It represented the farthest you could travel without dropping off the map. Jonah's destination choice shows us the desperation of his desire to forgo obeying God. He lived in a nation of people with a history of running from God. When things got challenging, they often chose to avoid or delay complete obedience.

> **Read the following passages and describe how God's people chose disobedience in each instance:**
>
> Exodus 32:1-4 *They made a golden idol to worship*
>
> Numbers 14:30-45 *They went up to the high hill country*
>
> **Recall the last time you sought to run from God's directions in your life. In the margin describe how "running" looked in your situation.**

Jonah followed the pattern of his countrymen—got clear divine directives he didn't want to follow and chose to disobey. He literally jumped ship and went to the nearest port in search of passage to take him to a place far away from the nagging voice of conviction.

## THE INSIDE RUNNER

While you and I might not have gone to such extremes to run from God externally, we've all run at one time or another in ways less noticeable. It's far more simple and discreet to run away internally, isn't it? We head to Tarshish in our hearts so we can still pretend we are obeying God.

We run mentally when we detach our thought life from our tasks and go through the motions. We run emotionally by building up a callousness displayed by the attitude we show to others. We can even run spiritually, going through the motions while having no fellowship with Him. We can be on the run from God's directives even while we are engrossed in them.

A friend I'll call Stella readily admits God led her to manage the children's program at her church, yet while she's busy doing, her heart's not in it. She's not giving 100 percent to God's call. She admits her heart and attitude are on a ship headed for Tarshish. She's upset at the problems she's faced and has grown weary of the program that doesn't seem to be making a difference. So she works but is not fully engaged. She's obeying God, but is this complete obedience?

Like Stella, you can be living life and yet be on the run from God, rebelliously pulling away from His will all the while. We can pack our internal bags just as quickly as Jonah packed his and be on a boat headed in the opposite direction of God's will even while we are in the throes of everyday life. But we must be careful. What is inside will eventually show up outside.

**Are you an "inside runner" in some area? If so, what are you running from and how is this evident in your life?**

*Trying to trust God in the midst of financial struggles*

**Read each verse in the margin. How is "internal running" illustrated in each verse?**

*Peopl*

**Isaiah 29:13**

*People worship the Lord, but their hearts aren't in it.*

**Acts 7:39**

*The Israelites rejected the Lord and in their hearts turned back to Egypt*

## OUR PLEDGE OF ALLEGIANCE

A closer look at why Jonah didn't want to obey God reveals something very interesting. Remember, Jonah had a deep love for his people. He was a devoted countryman who had an allegiance to his country. He wanted them to continue to flourish and their enemies to continue to flounder.

**According to Jonah 3:10–4:2, what did Jonah think would happen if he obeyed God and went to Nineveh?**

*He thought the Lord would show them mercy*

**Jonah's primary reasons for not wanting to preach in Nineveh were (choose all that apply):**
☒ fear for his life
⊘ not wanting Nineveh to receive mercy
⊘ allegiance to Israel
○ didn't like the climate

Jonah likely felt justified since going to Nineveh seemed contrary to God's plans for Israel. Until now he'd been commissioned by God to prophesy the expansion and prosperity of Israel since they alone were God's chosen nation and in their estimation, the only one worthy of His mercy. Nineveh becoming a recipient of that mercy seemed contrary to that goal.

*"Then the Lord said, 'because this people draw near with their words and honor Me with their lip service, but they remove their hearts far from Me, and their reverence for Me consists of tradition learned by rote.' "*
**Isaiah 29:13**

*"Our fathers were unwilling to be obedient to him, but repudiated him and in their hearts turned back to Egypt."*
**Acts 7:39**

**Have you ever felt justified in choosing not to obey God? Don't answer too quickly. Really think about it and explain your answer in the margin.**

Jonah was an elitist and hypernationalist. He was a patriot so dedicated to his people that he saw obedience to God's intervention as contrary to that loyalty. In actuality he had pledged allegiance not to God but to his people.

We too have pledged allegiance to something or someone. A way to determine where our allegiance lies is to consider how we respond to a divine intervention. Will we go with God even when He is calling us to our Nineveh, even if Nineveh goes against everything we thought we'd be doing? Sometimes heeding divine intervention requires breaking with that to which we have pledged our allegiance.

**End today by honestly considering to what you have pledged allegiance. Do ambitions, goals, people, or ideals have more of your commitment and loyalty than God does? Talk to Him about what you discover.**

## Day 2
# NOWHERE TO HIDE

*"Where can I go from Your Spirit? Or where can I flee from Your presence?" Psalm 139:7*

A recent devotional I ran across is a collection of daily readings that compiles Scripture and puts them in first person as if God's voice is speaking directly to you. Yesterday I read:

I am all around you, hovering over you even as you seek My Face. I am nearer than you dare believe, closer than the air you breathe. If My children could only recognize My Presence, they would never feel lonely again. I know every thought before you think it, every word before you speak it. My Presence impinges on your innermost being. Can you see the absurdity of trying to hide anything from Me? You can easily deceive other people, and even yourself; but I read you like an open, large-print book.[1]

Ask the Holy Spirit to speak personally to you through the words of the devotional. Go back and underline the phrases God uses most to speak to you.

As I've considered Jonah's flight to Tarshish, it occurred to me that he could have used simpler ways to avoid Nineveh. For instance, he could have chosen to simply stay where he was. Remaining in his home in Israel with his native people would have been an easier way to steer clear of the Assyrian nation. Most disobedience involves just that—a simple choice to stay put. Jonah also could have chosen to flee in a less extravagant way. Other cities would have been much easier and far less costly destinations.

While both of these options would have been equally disobedient, they would have required a lot less effort than paying a fare to go all the way to Tarshish. If he did charter the entire boat, the expense was steep. Whatever the exact circumstances, you can know it cost Jonah a lot of time, energy, effort, and resources to go to Tarshish.

> Most disobedience involves a simple choice to stay put.

If you were Jonah, which option would you have chosen? Why?

- ☒ stay in my home in Israel and lock the door
- ○ hop in my chariot and head for a friend's house in a neighboring town
- ○ get a one-way ticket to the most distant spot on earth

As you consider what God wants you to yield to right now, what choice would represent:

staying put— *Do nothing to try to find work — refuse to do my part to help.*

going, but not all the way— *Take whatever job I get offered, even though I don't like the job*

running in the opposite direction—
*try to take charge of the situation — refuse to trust that God will take care of it*

Jonah chose to run to the farthest destination he could fathom. Why? What was he trying to get away from?

*He was trying to Run from God and His presence*

Underline the repeated phrase in the verse in the margin.

*"he went down"*

> "Jonah rose up to flee to Tarshish from the presence of the LORD. So he went down to Joppa, found a ship which was going to Tarshish, paid the fare and went down into it to go with them to Tarshish from the presence of the LORD."
> Jonah 1:3

Jonah was
not merely
running from
someplace;
he was
trying to
run from
Someone.

Jonah was not merely running from someplace; he was trying to run from Someone. He wanted to put distance between himself and the One with the ticket to Nineveh. Yet Jonah was no newbie. He knew the workings of the Lord. He knew God could not be escaped. It's Religion 101. And Jonah was one of a rare breed of men called to be prophets. Fewer than 50 prophets existed in Israel from the time of Moses to Malachi. These men were "chosen for their sensitivity to God. Jonah must have been an impressive man, steeped in wisdom and insight, walking closely with the Lord."[2]

Jonah knew the truth about God. He knew running from God was futile. God is omnipresent, which means He's everywhere at the same time, no less in one location than in another. All of God is where you are, every moment of every day. So why did Jonah even bother to run? In Jonah 1:3, the original Hebrew phrase "from the presence of the LORD" is the word *milliphne*. This word was used when a person came out of an official audience with the king. In Genesis 41:46, this same word is used in reference to Joseph as he went out "from the presence of" Pharaoh into the entire land of Egypt.[3]

The implication is that Jonah was not simply running from the Lord. He would have known this to have been an impossibility; he was trying to steer clear of having a one-on-one, face-to-face encounter with Him. Jonah wanted to put distance between himself and the place where God's tangible presence rested with His people. In other words, he didn't want to sense God's nearness. He didn't want to hear His voice or have an awareness of His presence.

First Kings 8 gives us further insight. It tells of the dedication of the temple (see 8:6-12,27-30). God made special promises regarding His presence and the temple.

**What does 1 Kings 9:3 teach about God's presence and the temple?**

*God said His eyes & heart would be there forever - the temple was consecrated*

Jerusalem was the epicenter of Jewish life for many reasons. It served as the hub of economic and social needs. It was also the place where God's presence rested. It was this presence from which Jonah wanted to run.

**If you were in a season of rebellion against God, which of these might you try to avoid? In the margin note why.**

- ⊘ group Bible study
- ⊘ personal Bible study
- ⊘ church
- ⊘ fellowship with strong Christian friends
- ⊘ other  *prayer*

*I'd try to avoid Anything that might make me feel God's presence or make me feel closer to Him*

# THE TRUTH ABOUT GOD

The omnipresence of God is wondrous. While He is ever-present, He reveals Himself more fully and tangibly at certain times and places. For example, 2 Kings 17 chronicles a time when Israel turned from God, sinned against Him, and rebelled without concern for the One who had freed them from Egypt.

**What common consequence mentioned in each verse of 2 Kings 17:18,20,23 did the people of God receive for their rebellion?** *They were removed from His presence. they were rejected, afflicted, given to plunderers, exiled*

This phrase basically means that they were deported from the place where God's presence was guaranteed and experienced. When taken into exile by their enemies, they were certainly still recipients of the omnipresence of God and yet had been removed from the place where God's manifest presence was on display. This is what Jonah was running from. He wanted to put distance between himself and God's manifest presence. Hearing the voice of God and sensing a nearness to His presence was too convicting.

When we flee from God's presence, we do a most unusual thing. We put ourselves in the very spot of punishment. We find the people who are most subject to bad consequences, and we join them in their negative results.

**Can you identify? Have you ever picked yourself up and dropped yourself into a negative situation by seeking to run from God?**

Knowledge of God's nearness can be most comforting to anyone seeking an intimate relationship with Him, and yet it can be the most burdensome reminder for the one who is seeking to avoid His direction and correction.

Yesterday I asked my oldest son Jackson to help me straighten up the bathroom. He was immersed in one of his favorite cartoons and didn't want to be interrupted. While he knew that he couldn't completely get away from me, he did go to his room, sit in his closet next to his toy box, and play. When I went looking for him, I was surprised to find him tucked away in that little cubbyhole. Jackson didn't mind being in the house with me as long as there was no "official audience." He didn't want *milliphne*—to see my eyes staring at him or hear my voice giving him directions again. He wanted distance between himself and my presence.

Jonah wanted the same. He separated himself from the promised land where he knew the active, dynamic, and intrusive voice of God would be.

**Right now is the knowledge of God's ubiquitous presence comforting or discomforting to you? Why?**

It is comforting - I have to believe He is in control of my finances & trust Him

God's continuous presence is a soothing balm to the hurting. His presence is also a scorching fire to those living in disobedience. One of the ways we can determine whether we are in right relationship with Him is to consider the way we feel about His closeness to us. Do we welcome it or are we trying to steer clear of it?

**Do you desire for God's presence to be manifested, or are you avoiding an encounter with Him?**

I would love to know what God wants me to do, but it isn't clear to me.

**How does this show up in your life?**

I pray, go to church, & Bible study & small group to understand His presence better & for fellowship

As you conclude today's lesson, consider this: Jonah was involved in ministry as a prophet to Israel and yet, when divinely interrupted, chose to run from God's manifest presence. He claimed loyalty to God and yet desired no intimate relationship with Him. Right now, you are taking part in a Bible study, fellowshiping with other believers (if you are doing this in a group) and probably participating in other good, religious activities. Are you in any way doing good things while at the same time avoiding a close, intimate relationship with the Lord?

**Journal your thoughts.**

I still struggle with trusting God completely in my finances. I know He never will forsake me, but I still struggle w/ human fears & anxieties.

# ON THE WAY DOWN

*"Don't you realize that whatever you choose to obey becomes your master? You can choose sin, which leads to death, or you can choose to obey God and receive his approval." Roman 6:16, NLT*

It wasn't this bad in the beginning.

That's what she told me in our first meeting. I sat across from her in the transitional home where she lived and listened to the chapters of her life unfold like a bad movie. It was a tale of a life out of control. She'd struggled through an addiction, countless illicit relationships, and a host of other horrid decisions that had left her with a crippled life and an aching heart.

As she shared her saga, she almost seemed unable to believe the path her life had taken. Ultimately, she leaned back in her chair, stared blankly out the window, and almost whispered, "If I'd only known where those first bad decisions would have led me, maybe I would have chosen differently."

Those first decisions. Those first choices. They are critical.

I wasn't my parents' easiest child. If they were up with worry at night, it was probably because of something I said or did. I had a sassy streak of rebellion that ran deep, and when I was caught in disobedience, my tendency was to try to lie myself out of trouble. I was always amazed at how quickly and easily one lie had to become two and then that second one had to be parlayed into a third. Lies became one slippery slope after another that took me to an edge where I'd teeter, with no way out except down.

> **Can you recall the last time one decision led you on a downward spiral of rebellion or bad decisions? In the margin jot a few details and prepare to discuss them with your group this week.**

Jonah knew a thing or two about the downward spiral of disobedience. According to Jonah 1:3, it began with running from God. The descent down a slippery slope culminated in chapter 2 at the bottom of the sea.

When he first started running, Jonah in essence stepped down from his prophetic office and went down to Joppa—geographically downhill. He found a ship and went down to it. His descent didn't stop there. Once on board he went down into the hold to get some sleep (1:5).

Do you see the pattern here? His decision to run from God's command and to escape God's manifest presence spun a web of disaster from which he couldn't get free. Before he knew it, the circumstances gained momentum and took on a life of their own.

**Read the following verses and write a few key words to summarize how Jonah's circumstances escalated.**

Jonah 1:4 *A violent storm arose at sea*

Jonah 1:7 *The sailors drew lots to see who was responsible - the lot fell to Jonah*

Jonah 1:15 *Jonah was thrown overboard*

Jonah 1:17 *Jonah was swallowed by a great fish*

## DOWN AND OUT

King David is one of the most phenomenal characters in the Bible. From his childhood until his death, his story has captured the attention of millions, inspiring them to live bravely and boldly for God. Yet this man had no clean record. If anyone knows how a few bad decisions can make a huge mess to clean up, it's David.

His downhill descent began in 2 Samuel 11. It was springtime, and he was king of Israel. While other kings went out to war, David chose to stay home in Jerusalem. I don't know why he stayed home or what happened to get him out of bed that fateful night, but he threw the covers back and decided to get some fresh air on his rooftop. And that's when he saw her. She was gorgeous, and she was taking a bath. Talk about a romantic setting! Just imagine—a moonlit starry night, an undressed woman, and a lonely king—a recipe for disaster. David could have gone back to his room and tried to clear his head, but he didn't.

**From the verses in the margin chronicle the steps in David's downward spiral.**

David's deception ran deep and culminated in a pregnancy and a murder. I wonder how stunned David was as he considered the recent events of his life. Did he wonder how things had gotten so out of control?

Step 1:
2 Samuel 11:3
*David saw Bathsheba, and asked for info about her*

Step 2:
2 Samuel 11:4-5
*David sent for her. He slept w/ her & she became pregnant*

Step 3:
2 Samuel 11:6-13
*David tries to get Uriah to go home & sleep w/ Bathsheba to cover his adultery, but he won't go.*

Step 4:
2 Samuel 11:14-15, 17
*David asks Joab to arrange Uriah's death in battle*

Step 5:
2 Samuel 11:27
*after Uriah's death David & Bathsheba, but the Lord is displeased w/ David's sins*

We see another illustration of bad choices running rampant in a person's life in the story of the prodigal son (Luke 15:11-32). In this stunning picture of a father and his beloved children, we meet a son who willingly chose to take the good gifts he had been given and leave the safety of his home and the love of his father. Like Jonah, he set his sights on a "distant country" and lived rebelliously. It was not until his downward tumble gained steam and he found himself desiring the slop he was serving up to some pigs that it occurred to him how far he had fallen.

> **Earlier you wrote about a time your circumstances got out of control due to your bad decisions. What was the "pigsty" experience where you were at your lowest?**

During college I lived in rebellion against God in many ways. In one case, I developed a relationship with a young man who was not a Christian. While I told him I couldn't be serious because he didn't know the Lord, my actions said the contrary. I spent a lot of time with him and allowed our relationship to grow. Before I knew it, I was attached emotionally and seemed to be on a roller coaster I couldn't get off no matter how I tried.

How clearly I remember a date with him one evening. We ended up at one of his friend's homes. When we pulled into the driveway, I knew I was in the wrong place. Rows of cars were lined up and a party was underway. Liquor bottles peppered the lawn and cigarette butts lay everywhere. Vulgar music blasted through the windows and the smell of drugs was in the air.

He grabbed my hand and took me in. Too embarrassed and cowardly to say anything, I plastered on a smile as he introduced me to his friends. I was offered a drink of this and a smoke of that. For the first time in my friendship with this young man, I was uncomfortable. I looked around and wondered, *How did I end up here?* The answer lay in my very first decision to allow a relationship that should never have been.

> **Read James 1:14-15 in the margin. Underline the stages of the descent of disobedience as outlined in this verse.**
>
> temptation → sin → death
>
> **From the personal circumstance you mentioned earlier, how have you seen these stages unfold?**

*"But each one is tempted when he is carried away and enticed by his own lust. Then when lust has conceived, it gives birth to sin; and when sin is accomplished, it brings forth death."*
**James 1:14-15**

The decisions you are making today will impact your tomorrows. How you choose to respond to God's leading right now will determine how your future unfolds. Every "David" will end up in a web of deception. Every prodigal will find himself in a pigsty, and every Jonah will look up and see storm clouds gathering. It's only a matter of time.

What is God asking of you today? Are you responding with willingness or by running for Joppa, looking for a boat to get away from God's will? Don't head down. Look up. God's best for you is on the horizon.

## LOOKING UP

While I was horrified to be at that party those many years ago, looking back I am thankful for it. Had I not had that eye-opening moment, I might have stayed blindly in the relationship longer than I did. That moment shook me awake from the emotional trance I'd been in. It brought me back to my senses again. Sometimes that's what it takes when you are down— to be jolted awake to start looking up again. For the prodigal, God used a pigpen (Luke 15:14-17), for Jonah a fish (Jonah 1:15,17).

> **What low moment for David got him to realize his need? (See 2 Sam. 12:1-7,15,19-20.)**
>
> - Nathan rebukes him
> - David & Bathsheba's child was stricken w/illness by the Lord & dies
>
> **How did God use your "pigsty" experience to bring you back to your senses?**

If you have made bad choices and found yourself on a descent that has led you places you'd never thought you'd go, today is a good day to begin an upward climb. As you saw from the examples above, sin has consequences. Yet while God is a God of justice, He is also compassionate. So, look up. When you do, you'll see the eyes of a merciful Father looking back with open arms to gather you back to Himself.

> "The LORD longs to be gracious to you, and therefore He waits on high to have compassion on you. For the LORD is a God of justice; How blessed are all those who long for Him" (Isa. 30:18).

Day 4

# THE SLEEPER

*"But Jonah had gone below into the hold of the ship,
lain down, and fallen sound asleep." Jonah 1:5*

The other day I sat down on the couch for a moment of rest. I told my sons to allow me 15 minutes to relax and then we could continue the day's play. My good intentions didn't translate into action. One hour later I was shocked to discover I'd fallen asleep and looked up to find three little people within an inch of my nose peering down at me.

Interesting how you can be asleep and not realize it until you've awakened. I wonder if Jonah realized that's exactly what he'd done.

Thank God for the storm. Not something you'd expect to say—thank God for stormy patches in your life. But in Jonah's case, had there not been a storm, the captain may not have roused sleeping Jonah. Then he might have stayed below deck, undisturbed all the way to Tarshish.

So thank God for the storm not just for Jonah but anytime we're on our way out of God's will too. You can be asleep and not realize it until a storm shakes you awake from your spiritual slumber. Yesterday we considered the downward spiral of disobedience. Today let's consider the affect it had on Jonah. Have you ever wondered how he could sleep in a storm that terrified everyone else? While they were reeling from the chaos around them, Jonah was cuddled up in the hull to catch a nap. How could that be?

> **Which option do you think best explains Jonah's actions? He slept because:**
> ⊘ He was exhausted from running away.
> ◯ He felt justified in going to Tarshish.
> ◯ He knew the storm was a consequence from Yahweh.
> ⊗ His heart was hardened, and he was numb.
> — ⊘ He wanted to "sleep away" the conviction.
> ◯ Other _____

While the text does not specify why Jonah slept, commentators suggest any of the above could be possible. It had been a long day. Jonah made a trip to Joppa, organized the charter of a boat, and guilt has a way of affecting you physically (Ps. 32:1-5). He could have just been extremely tired, or he could have wanted to sleep away his sin and accompanying conviction.

I've certainly done that at times, hoping when I woke up everything would go back to normal.

Possibly Jonah slept because he knew the storm was from God and he just gave up and settled into the consequences to let God do whatever He may. Or maybe Jonah felt his decision was warranted and understandable. He could have slept with ease because he genuinely felt what he was doing was right. While all of these could be correct, my mother-sense tells me there's a bit more to it. You see, as a mother of small children, I am often overwhelmingly tired at the end of a long day. Yet if any of them makes even the slightest peep in the middle of the night, I am on my feet and in their rooms to check on them. Why? I have such a love for them and deep sensitivity to their needs that exhaustion doesn't (always) keep me from responding.

I can't help but wonder if Jonah's justification led to a lack of sensitivity to God. After all, "the hardening of a tender heart almost always starts with a justifiable action."[4] Was a hardened heart the real reason Jonah slept through such a tumultuous storm? Was he too calloused to God's desires, His prompting and even His correction to take note of the storm? He was, after all, on a run from God not only with his feet but with his heart as well.

**Recall a time when you slept through God's movement in your life. What was your reason:**
- ◯ I was too exhausted to respond.
- ◯ I felt justified in my actions.
- ◯ I knew the storm was my consequence so I just didn't put up a fight.
- ◯ Looking back, I realize my heart was a bit hard and desensitized to God's Spirit.
- ◯ I wanted to ignore conviction and hoped everything would change when I woke up.
- ⊘ Other _wasn't sure what I was supposed to do_

**Missionary Assignment**

As a group, determine some of the indicators that the church has fallen asleep in regards to the lost. In recent years, what "storms" do you think the Spirit has sent to awaken God's people?

Jonah's storm on the sea is not unlike the storm of conviction the Holy Spirit sends when we are traveling out of God's will. Thank God for the storm He sends to wake us from our spiritual slumber. Whether we are sleeping through a season of sin because of exhaustion, disobedience we've justified, or hard-heartedness, His Spirit will send storm clouds in an attempt to awaken us and help us come back to our senses.

Remaining sensitive to God's work is a necessity if we are to respond, yet it's difficult to maintain when we are living in rebellion. In Jonah's case, the storm itself did not stir his hardened heart, but it did compel the pagan chief petty officer to go down and wake him up. The captain figured that they needed all the help they could get. Their calls to numerous gods were not yielding a response, so they wanted Jonah to join them in pursuit of a god who would have sympathy on their plight.

> **What irony do you see in the exchange between the captain and Jonah in 1:5-6?** *a pagan captain is asking a Christian to pray*
>
> **For group discussion later, jot down some thoughts on how a pagan man waking a believing man to pray correlates to the world and the church in modern times.**

## JUST CALL IT LOVE

My parents disciplined me. I might as well come clean and tell you that I gave them cause to discipline me often, probably more than all my other siblings put together. I remember after a spanking or being grounded in older years, my father would always look at me with sweet, caring eyes and say, "I discipline you because I love you."

I didn't get it.

Only now that I have children of my own do I have a bit of an understanding about what they meant. Discipline is a sign of love for my children. When they stray, my love for them allows a storm to set them straight and get them back on track. Likewise, the storm of consequences the Lord may have allowed in your life is a sign of His great affection for you. Any time you've trailed off course, the winds and the waves you faced showed His care. According to Hebrews, divine discipline is a sign of more than just His love.

*"My Son, do not regard lightly the discipline of the Lord, nor faint when you are reproved by Him. For those whom the Lord loves He disciplines and He scourges every son whom He receives."*
**Hebrews 12:5-6**

> **What else does divine discipline reveal (Heb. 12:7-8)?** *God is treating you like His beloved child*

The other day I heard a young girl in the grocery store line back talking her mother. I couldn't believe the harsh and disrespectful way she was speaking to her mom. I'm a simple southern girl who believes that kids should honor their parents, so it took all of my restraint not to turn around, grab that girl's chin in my hands, squeeze a bit, and tell her to apologize.

I didn't do it for one simple reason: She's not my child.

Have you ever been upset because someone else seems to be "getting away with it"? They are knee-deep in a lifestyle of sin, and it seems to be going unnoticed. It could be because they aren't His. So "do not fret because of evildoers. Be not envious toward wrongdoers" (Ps. 37:1). The Lord's discipline in your life is a sign of His relationship with you. It's a privilege. He admonishes you because you are His.

> Read Psalm 89:30-33 in the margin. Underline the word "sons." Circle the portions that reveal divine discipline and put an asterisk next to the portions that confirm His love in the midst of that discipline.

*"If his sons forsake My law and do not walk in My judgments, if they violate My statutes and do not keep My commandments, then I will punish their transgression with the rod and their iniquity with stripes. But I will not break off My lovingkindness from him, nor deal falsely in My faithfulness."*
**Psalm 89:30-33**

## HEAR THE ALARM

It's time for us to wake up. The Spirit's seeking to rouse you and me, the body of Christ, so we can get busy. Maybe you've not even been aware of that fact that you've been sleeping. Maybe this study on the prophet who slept or just this particular lesson is precisely what God will use to stir you.

The world, with its pagan thoughts and ideals, shouldn't have to rouse us back to intimacy with the one true God. Rather, the soft stirring of the Spirit's conviction in us should be enough to cause us to "Awake, sleeper, and arise from the dead, and Christ will shine on you" (Eph. 5:14).

Day 5

# THE GREAT EXCHANGE

*"The vessel that he was making of clay was spoiled in the hand of the potter; so he remade it into another vessel, as it pleased the potter to make." Jeremiah 18:4*

I've become a master at making leftovers into gourmet meals. I wish I had Paula Deen's charm and Rachael Ray's sensibility while doing it, but most often I'm bumping into my kids, slamming cabinet doors, and searching the refrigerator for anything that doesn't have mold on it from being forgotten at the bottom back corner. Yes, one day I aspire to cook each meal like those women do—like my mother does—with a smile on my face, a crisp white apron on, fresh ingredients and newly minted recipes. Until then, I'll just do the best I can.

Do I hear an Amen?

About two kids ago I stopped trying to be Chef Boyardee® every night and started fishing out things I'd already cooked to reuse. (Dave Ramsey would call this good financial stewardship.) I've become a gourmet leftover chef. I dice and chop and reconfigure. Then I top the day-old meat and vegetables with cream of mushroom soup and inevitably some grated cheese. Bake it at 350 degrees for a bit, give it a French-sounding name and voilà! My family thinks I've really gone and done something special.

Ahhhh. Applause please.

God's good at taking our messes, our leftovers, and doing something good with them. Parts of all of our lives we'd just as soon forget, yet in the hands of a Master, our mess can become the greatest miracle of all. He has a way of chopping, dicing, and reconfiguring the parts that we thought were of no use. He's got a knack for pouring on His Spirit and sprinkling on a bit of grace and mercy. Then, voilà! Fresh out of the oven of a trial or two, there's something delicious from your life that you never thought possible.

Ahhhh. Applause please.

Just ask Jonah. Between justified disobedience, a hardened conscience, the ferocious storm of discipline, the frightening waves and the stares of those sailors peering down at him, I'm sure he never thought anything good was going to come out of this. But, indeed, something would.

**In 1:14-16 what did the sailors do that they had likely never done before (v. 14)? What actions did they take (v. 16)?**

*Prayed to God for forgiveness.*
*offered a sacrifice to the Lord & made vows to him*

These sailors were most likely Phoenicians who were "responsible for most of the sea traffic in the Mediterranean during the first half of the first millennium BC. It was they who pioneered exploration and trade by sea."[5] These men were pagans who came from a polytheistic culture. They worshiped numerous gods. Each god governed a different part of nature and was easily offended. When trouble arose, they never knew who had done wrong or which god had been offended. So when they became afraid by the storm, "every man cried to his god" (v. 5) in an effort to make amends and tidy up any spiritual messes they may have unknowingly made.

The sailors prayed to Jonah's God by the specific covenant name *Yahweh*. Since these men were polytheists, the use of the name designated for the one true God is noteworthy. It means they recognized a difference between this God and the ones to whom they had previously prayed. Jonah's rebellion, the violent storm, and their fear all played a role in causing their attention to be turned to the God of Abraham, Isaac, and Jacob.

**Have you ever been surprised by how God allowed good to come out of a time of rebellion in your life? What did God accomplish?**

*Not rebellion - I came out of divorce stronger & wiser & closer to God*

Several years ago a man walked up to me at a banquet. He had a familiar face, but I couldn't quite place him. He said we'd gone to the same college and that on one occasion I'd witnessed to him. He reminded me that he'd not responded at that time and that I'd gone away from him in despair. He wanted me to know that I planted a seed during those years. Now he was following the Lord in full time ministry. I was awe struck and encouraged. Not because of anything I'd done but because God had been able to bring something honorable out of that season of my life.

## MOVING WATERS AND MOVING HEARTS

Note Jonah 1:9-10 in the margin. Yesterday we saw an unbeliever have to ask the believer to pray. Groggy from his nap, you'd think at that point Jonah might have come clean about who he was, where he was from, and where he was going, but he didn't. They had to cast lots to determine what they should do next.

Would Jonah then decide to spill the beans? Nope. Not until the lot fell on Jonah and all eyes turned in his direction did he crumble under their scrutiny and finally tell them who his God was and that he was running from Him. In the midst of all that was happening, I can't help but wonder if Jonah—the Israelite and the prophet—was ashamed to speak the name of his God in conjunction with his own.

*"He said to them, 'I am a Hebrew, and I fear the LORD God of heaven who made the sea and the dry land.' Then the men became extremely frightened and they said to him, 'How could you do this?' For the men knew that he was fleeing from the presence of the LORD, because he had told them."*
**Jonah 1:9-10**

**What details about their current circumstances and Jonah's description of his God in Jonah 1:9 may have begun to change the sailors' hearts?**

*"God of heaven who made the sea"*

**Have you ever been embarrassed to reveal to someone who your God is once she has seen the way you've acted? If so, what were the circumstances?**

*I wasn't asked to reveal, but I'd have embarrassed to admit it after acting rudely to another*

I wonder if Jonah's heart was palpitating when he came clean. Here he was running from God—and not just any God but the God of Israel who made the sea on which they were being tossed. Though the sailors' introduction to Yahweh wasn't under the best evangelistic circumstances, events were set in place for their conversion. For no god they called to could fix their circumstances, yet Jonah's God was the One who not only ruled but created the sea. Immediately, their prayer lives changed.

The sailors' use of Yahweh's covenant name through the latter half of chapter 1 shows the awe with which they revered this God from whom Jonah had the nerve to rebel. Can you imagine how their wonder escalated when, after throwing Jonah overboard, the sea became calm immediately? Yahweh had proven Himself to be a God of wonders who deserved to be worshiped and obeyed. In fact, they were so stunned by this awesome God that they begged Him to have mercy on them for throwing Jonah overboard when all of the other options for saving themselves had been exhausted. Again, these pagans had regard for human life when Jonah, the believer, had no regard for the lives of the Ninevites.

Read Jonah 1:14-16 and take note of each time the sailors used the covenant name "LORD."

**Has an unbeliever ever done something that shamed you because it was more Christlike than what you'd done? What affect did this have on you?**

*Yes, and it made me want to model their example*

God had even orchestrated Jonah's life, Jonah's rebellion, and Jonah's consequences so that they would be tools needed to convert sinners. The storm created by Jonah's rebellion was the perfect backdrop for them to meet the one true God, the One who governed the sea.

Do you think a season of your life held wasted years with no redeeming qualities? God can use anything. He's the Master of taking the bits and pieces of our leftovers and making something amazing out of it. He gives "beauty for ashes, the oil of joy for mourning, the garment of praise for the spirit of heaviness" so that He might be glorified (Isa. 61:3, NKJV). Have you, like Jonah, mishandled the divine interruptions that have come your way? God can use anything, even the leftovers, for His glory.

**Note this week's navigation tools.**

**Day 1** *our response to intervention indicates where our loyalty lies - we can run on the inside*

**Day 2** *Are we running from relationship w/ God?*

**Day 3** *One bad decision can start a downward spiral*

**Day 4** *intervention can be God's way of waking us up*

**Day 5** *God can take your storm or wasted years & use it for Good*

# Session 3
## VIEWER GUIDE

*When God shakes you up, you find out what's in you, because when you're shaken, what's in you comes out*

The Holy Spirit's job is to <u>SANCtify</u> us.

The more vast the <u>Consequences</u> you've had
to bear, the more <u>VAST</u> the work He has planned for
you afterward.

God isn't out to <u>hurt</u> you; He's out to <u>Redeem</u> you.

*God doesn't leave us stuck in a mess just for fun, he allows it to grow us*

"Then Jonah prayed to the LORD his God from the stomach of the fish" (Jonah 2:1).

*In the midst of our consequences (feeling guilty, etc), we have an opportunity to be Restored to Relationship w/God and call out to Him*

FOR THOSE WHOM THE LORD LOVES HE DISCIPLINES, AND HE SCOURGES EVERY
SON WHOM HE RECEIVES" (Heb. 12:6).

"For You had cast me into the deep, into the heart of the seas, and the current
engulfed me. All Your breakers and billows passed over me. So I said, 'I have been
expelled from Your sight. Nevertheless I will look again toward Your holy temple.'
Water encompassed me to the point of death. The great deep engulfed me, weeds
were wrapped around my head. I descended to the roots of the mountains. The earth
with its bars was around me forever, but You have brought up my life from the pit,
O LORD my God" (Jonah 2:3-6).

*God wants to rescue us from the pit*

Now is your opportunity to <u>CAll</u> out to God.

*Reach out to God*

**The Holy Spirit extends to you an opportunity to be back in relationship with Him.**

*"And he said, 'I called out of my distress to the LORD, and He answered me. I cried for help from the depth of Sheol; You heard my voice' " (Jonah 2:2).*

Your ~~tears~~ are falling into the ___PALM___ of His ___hand___. – He cares

Micah 7:7 – God hears us when we pray

You serve a God who is ___waiting___ to ___hear___ from you, and He can't wait to ___Respond___.

*"Therefore the LORD longs to be gracious to you, and therefore He waits on high to have compassion on you. For the LORD is a God of justice; how blessed are all those who long for Him. O people in Zion, inhabitant in Jerusalem, you will weep no longer. He will surely be gracious to you at the sound of your cry; when He hears it, He will answer you" (Isa. 30:18-19).*

WEEK THREE

# Desperate Times, Desperate Measures

# NOW WHAT?

*"So they said to him, 'What should we do to you that the sea may become calm for us?'—for the sea was becoming increasingly stormy." Jonah 1:11*

The question hangs in the air after a mistake or problem. It swims through your mind when circumstances go haywire or when you fall into horrid consequences after rebellion. We must ask while we navigate this interrupted life: *What should we do?*

The storm raged around the sailors, threatening to break up the ship. These men needed answers. Since Jonah clearly told them he was running from God, they were sure that this storm was no simple act of nature. It had theological implications and was a deliberate act of Jonah's God. They wanted desperately to know, as we often do, how to navigate a life in turmoil.

We easily become paralyzed by fear or guilt when our lives seem to whirl out of control. A glimpse at our lives with all of their spinning parts can make us dizzy with disgust at the mess we may have made. It's easier to just sit, soak, and be sour. That's what the enemy would like. He'd prefer we get lazy, complacent, and apathetic with distance between ourselves and God's best. But if, like the sailors, we see the connection between our chaotic circumstances and our own decisions, we must ask, "Now what?"

> **What is your normal response when realizing that you are out of God's will and dealing with the consequences of bad decisions? Do you—**
> ○ become overwhelmed and paralyzed with guilt
> ○ rebel against the consequence and try to circumvent it
> ✓ settle in, accept the consequence, and learn from it
> ○ other _____

Maybe you're not currently in Jonah's position. I pray you're not. Hopefully, you've had a divine intervention and have chosen to yield to it, so you aren't in a state of rebellion against God's direction. If Jonah's situation doesn't apply to you, please stay with me. This week promises an important reminder of the redemptive truth of God's grace that mercifully rescues us anytime, anyplace, and in any situation.

Jonah's answers to the sailors' questions and subsequent actions give us a shadow of four significant New Testament principles for reconciling with God. We need to:

1. acknowledge our sin
2. accept God's discipline
3. ask for forgiveness
4. act on God's direction

**Which of the four principles do you find most difficult? Circle it, and note why you chose this one.**

*Sometimes it's hard to admit we've messed up*

Note that Jonah did not appear truly repentant for his actions. We'll see in chapter 4 that he still did not want God's mercy poured out on the Ninevites. However, his prayer in chapter 2 does suggest he realized the futility of running from God. While Jonah may not have fully realized the gravity of his disobedience, he was penitent. We can learn some critical lessons through his story about true repentance and its effects on us.

**Read these portions of Jonah and record any connection you see between the principle and Jonah's story.**

**acknowledge your sin—Jonah 1:12**
*Jonah admitted that the storm was his fault*
**accept the discipline—Jonah 1:15**
*He accepted being thrown overboard*
**ask for forgiveness—Jonah 2:2**
*He called to the Lord for help*
**act on God's direction—Jonah 2:9; 3:3**
*He vows to sacrifice & make good his word*

## PRINCIPLE #1—THE BLAME GAME

Jonah's response to the sailors' question in verse 11 illustrates the first move out of rebellion and back into the arms of God.

**Fill in the remaining portion of the verse:**
**"He said to them, 'Pick me up and throw me into the sea. Then the sea will become calm for you, for I know**
*It is my fault that this great* **' " (Jonah 1:12).**
*storm has come upon you.*

"I acknowledged my sin to You ... I said, 'I will confess my transgressions to the Lord'; and You forgave the guilt of my sin."
Psalm 32:5

Check all that apply. Jonah's statement seems to reveal that he …

- ☑ was taking responsibility for his actions and willing to accept the consequences
- ○ had figured a way out of having to follow God's will
- ☑ did not want the sailors to have to pay for his disobedience
- ○ was simply confessing that he knew the way to calm the storm
- ☑ was acknowledging that he had sinned

*He admitted fault & was willing to accept consequences (being thrown overboard) to keep the sailors from having to pay for his disobedience*

In the margin explain your selections.

The other day I was with my friend Paige who was visiting from out of town. I was driving her to a new restaurant in downtown Dallas. We'd called to get directions and were doing our best to navigate all of the one-way city streets. I was doing OK until I got tangled up in some construction. The old familiar signs I was used to following had been torn down and temporary ones put in their place. The strange signs, orange cones, and tape lacing the roadways got me a bit turned around. Suddenly I found myself back on the freeway I'd exited just moments before. Admittedly, I was a bit embarrassed to tell to her that I was going the wrong way, but if we ever wanted to sit down for dinner, I had to acknowledge the wrong turn I'd taken. Getting back on track depended on it.

What would be your tendency in a situation like that?
- ○ I'd blame the restaurant for not giving better directions or at least warning me about the construction.
- ○ I'd be too frustrated at the time I'd wasted and just go somewhere else to eat dinner.
- ○ I'm directionally challenged. I wouldn't even know I was going the wrong way.
- ☑ I'd tell my friend I was sorry, take the first exit, and turn around immediately.
- ☑ other  *I probably would have had my GPS w/me to redirect me*

How does your choice compare to how you act when you realize you are going the wrong direction in life?

*Pretty similar*

*"He who conceals his transgressions will not prosper, but he who confesses and forsakes them will find compassion."*
**Proverbs 28:13**

What spiritual signs do you think you can look for that reveal you are headed in the wrong direction? Plan to discuss this question with your group this week.

*When it feels like you are struggling instead of feeling like you are in harmony w/what you're supposed to be doing (everything comes together)*

## ALL THE RIGHT SIGNS

As we tried to navigate our way to the restaurant that night, it wasn't a road mark that first warned me of the wrong direction. As I sped back up on the freeway, I just "knew" that something didn't feel right about the direction I'd chosen. I've lived in Dallas all my life and have grown fairly accustomed to the neighborhoods surrounding the downtown area. Without seeing any particular road mark, my internal compass just didn't feel right. Sure enough, posted signs verified what I sensed was true.

I can't help but think that the change in Jonah's path from the road of rebellion to the pathway of penitence began long before he sat waterlogged in the belly of the fish. In fact, it began even before he was tossed overboard.

What were the sailors' five questions (Jonah 1:8)?

1. *Who is responsible for this trouble?*

2. *What do you do?*

3. *Where do you come from?*

4. *What is your country?*

5. *From what people are you?*

Consider Jonah's response (v. 9). What part of Jonah's reply is not an answer to a question he was asked?

*"I worship the Lord, the God of Heaven"*

What else does the text reveal that he told the sailors?

*- He is a Hebrew*
*- His God made the sea & land*

Jonah didn't answer all the questions, but the truth of those answers most likely swam around in his heart and head as he pondered the sailors' penetrating inquiries. The reality of who he was and what he was doing must have felt like a searing weight on his rebellious conscience.

As Jonah responded to the questions of the frightened Phoenician sailors, he simply stated that he was a Hebrew. He chose the word commonly used to distinguish the people of God from those of other nations. In fact, Gentiles would often use the term *Hebrew* as a way of differentiating between themselves and those who served Yahweh and were beneficiaries of the covenant relationship.

No doubt, just the name reminded Jonah of the gravity of his unique connection with the one true God. The ministry of God's Spirit evidently washed over Jonah. His heart was overwhelmed with conviction, and he proceeded to spill out a laundry list of adjectives to describe the God who governed his people and who governed him.

With the storm still raging on the sea, another storm raged in the prophet. With each word of truth, his heart was pierced. His journey back home—to right relationship with God and His will—had begun.

**Read Isaiah 30:21 in the margin. Summarize it below.**

*Whenever you stray from the path, God's word will tell you the way to walk*

**Recall a time when your return to fellowship with God was spurred on by internal conviction through God's Word. In the margin describe this conviction and how it compelled you to obedience.**

*"Your ears will hear a word behind you, 'This is the way, walk in it,' whenever you turn to the right or to the left."*
Isaiah 30:21

## THE FINE ART OF ASKING QUESTIONS

God's Spirit is a master at asking questions. He has a way of challenging us to consider where we've been, what we've done, and how we plan to make right anything we may be doing wrong. Our journey back to the Lord begins when we take time to consider and accept the conviction He uses to stir us and awaken us to the new direction He wants for us.

Even if we are not in a season of known rebellion like Jonah was, it is always in our best interest to pray like the psalmist prayed: "Search me, O God, and know my heart; test me and know my anxious thoughts. Point out anything in me that offends you, and lead me along the path of everlasting life" (Ps. 139:23-24, NLT).

**Take time to ask God to give you all the right signs. Record any questions He might be raising in your heart and consider your answer to each one. Acknowledge any rebellion He might bring to your attention.**

# CASTAWAY

*"So they picked up Jonah and threw him into the*
*sea, and the sea stopped its raging." Jonah 1:15*

I'll never forget the day I met a kind woman by the name of Donna Otto. Her books had inspired me, and I was intrigued to be in her presence. I listened eagerly as we sat in rocking chairs on the porch of a retreat center in North Carolina. Her wisdom on how I could balance motherhood, ministry, and marriage was priceless. Our conversation ended with her challenging me not to think that every good opportunity that came along was God's will for me. She gave this illustration:

> You are in a hurry and waiting on a down elevator. One finally arrives, but is unbelievably full. The people inside can tell from the expression on your face that you really want to get on. So they shift to the left and the right, cramming themselves together just to give you some space to get on. You are right in the middle and all eyes are on you. When the elevator doors shut, the car starts moving—in the wrong direction. You need to go down and this elevator is going up. There you stand elbow to elbow in an uncomfortable crowd knowing full well that you need to get off, but you are frozen with humiliation. These people went out of their way to let you on. They made room for you. You can't bring yourself to let them see the mistake you made. So what do you do? Stay on and ride 22 more floors in the wrong direction or humbly admit your mistake and get off so you don't waste any time getting set in the right direction?

**What would you do in this situation?**
○ ride all the way up to the top floor
○ push a button for a lower floor so it can at least look
   like you need to get off
⊘ make a quick joke and hop off immediately
○ simply get off without worrying how it appears to others

**How does the hypothetical situation relate to how you react in real-life situations? (Respond in the margin.)**

- Probably the same
- Maybe I've mistakenly jumped at good opportunities that really weren't meant for me
- I hope I learned by experience not to "stay on the elevator" too long

Yesterday we discovered four principles to reconciliation with God. The first is to acknowledge our sin and accept blame for our actions—to get off the elevator headed in the wrong direction so we can get back in step with God's will for us.

**What is the second principle?**

*accept discipline*

# PRINCIPLE #2—MAN OVERBOARD

**Read Jonah 1:16. How might this verse read differently if the sailors were throwing you overboard?** *I would probably struggle*

By the time the sailors got around to tossing Jonah overboard, they'd become pretty used to hurling items into the sea. They'd mostly likely already thrown "precious metals, horses and mules, ivory, and various other products" into the Mediterranean.[1]

I'm amazed that Jonah so easily allowed the sailors to throw him into the ferocious waves. While I enjoy swimming with my kids and have even gotten on a boat or two, I have no interest in being hurled overboard from a vessel in a storm.

If I'd been in Jonah's shoes, I'd never have advised them to toss me overboard. Then if some overzealous shipmates decided to do it anyway, they'd have had to chase me all over the deck and capture me by force.

Since Jonah advised them to throw him overboard and no evidence suggests a struggle, it appears that he did not fight the correction God allowed. He learned experientially what he already knew deep down: he could not escape God. Now, he gave all of himself over to what the Lord was permitting. Finally, the prophet held nothing back, including his own body, and surrendered completely. God now had what He wanted in the first place—the prophet's willingness to obey. The fish became the way to preserve Jonah for the future ministry God had for him.

**David gave us insight into this second principle of reconciliation with God. Read Psalm 119:71,75 in the margin, and rewrite these verses in your own words.**

*David felt it was good that he was punished, so that he could learn God's laws, and that he knew God's judgements were righteous and that His punishment was done out of love & faithfulness*

*"It is good for me that I was afflicted, that I may learn Your statutes. ... I know, O LORD, that Your judgments are righteous, and that in faithfulness You have afflicted me."*
**Psalm 119:71,75**

**Is the Lord allowing divine discipline in your life right now? If so, are you yielding to it or fighting against it?**

*I'm not sure if this is divine discipline — my financial struggles are my own fault. I'm working on trusting God totally with it.*

## DISCIPLINE'S DESIGN

Last week we briefly considered Hebrews 12:6, which outlines the benefit of God's discipline. God allows reproof and correction as a sign of His love for us and His intention to use us. Divine discipline, reproof, and correction indicate that we have a relationship with Him. Make no mistake about it, His discipline has a method and specific design. His goal is to revive so that He can realign. Jonah's heart needed a realignment.

While God desired to dispense mercy to the Ninevites, Jonah wanted them demolished. His aspirations were not in sync with God's. The discipline God allowed was not meant to punish Jonah; it was meant to prepare him. Accepting and surrendering to divine discipline was in Jonah's best interest. Consider the divine design behind God's discipline.

> ## His goal is to revive so that He can realign.

**In light of Jonah's disregard for the lives of the Ninevites, what lesson might he have taken from Jonah 1:13?**

*The sailors tried to spare his life & show him mercy when Jonah had none for the Ninevites*

**What do you think the prophet should have learned from what took place in Jonah 1:17–2:10?**

*when he was at rock bottom he needed to admit his error in disobeying & have gratitude for the mercy he was shown & gladly keep his vows*

When Jerry and I discipline our sons, we try to make sure it is not in anger. While we aren't perfect at this, we try to take a deep breath, calm down, and make sure we have a design to our discipline. Our objective is always to mold and soften their hearts, not simply adjust their actions.

If I send one of the boys to his room, I'm hopeful that he'll take time to consider his actions, how they affected others and what he could have done differently. I want him to emerge with a willingness to apologize and change his behavior as a result of a malleable heart and attitude. I'm not as eager to make him a "good kid" now as much as I want him to be an upstanding adult later. Lasting change can only take place if his heart is engaged. In the activity above, I wonder if God intended the actions of the sailors in verse 13 to demonstrate that Gentiles are worthy of Jonah's concern.

Consider these two equations:

Behavioral Change – Heart Change = Temporary Change

Heart Change + Behavioral Change = Permanent Change

**Rewrite the principle of these equations in your own words in the margin.** *— If we △ outwardly but our heart isn't in it, △ is temporary — When we △ our outward behavior and our heart is in it, △ is permanent*

**How have you seen this in your own life or another's life? What have you or could you learn from it?** *If I or anyone else just "goes through the motions", the △ doesn't last and it is not sincere*

God's goal for us is that we mature into spiritual adults who have tender hearts that mirror His. He doesn't discipline for fun or for sport. He does so to prepare us for what He has in store.

God still wanted to use Jonah, and He still wants to use us. In fact, look at the great lengths God took to preserve Jonah and give him opportunity to participate in His purposes. He hurled a wind and a storm so fierce they almost destroyed the ship (v. 4), He gave the sailors no other option but to toss Jonah overboard (v. 15). Then God prepared a fish that would come by at just the right time to swallow him whole to keep him from drowning.

God's discipline was centered around the care of His beloved prophet. And His discipline in our lives is no different. Knowing this should cause us to be more willing to yield to the discomfort of the discipline He allows.

When we come to our study of the final chapter of Jonah, we'll see God still had His work cut out for Him when it came to this man, yet the transforming and revitalizing work of God's discipline had certainly begun. When Jonah found himself in the belly of the fish, he did something he hadn't done since leaving Israel. "Then Jonah prayed to the LORD his God from the stomach of the fish" (2:1).

Jonah prayed. He talked to God.

Open communication is one of the first signs of a heart being molded by God. Have you fallen into a place of hardship as a result of rebellion against God and the direction He's asked you to go? Are you trying to figure out what to do next while you seek to cope with life? Take Jonah's cue: Acknowledge your sin and accept the discipline. When you do, you'll find your heart changing within you, softening to the things of God.

**End today by opening the lines of communication with God. Spend a few moments in prayer.**

# OUT WITH THE OLD

*"If we [freely] admit that we have sinned and confess
our sins, He is faithful and just (true to His own nature
and promises) and will forgive our sins [dismiss our
lawlessness] and [continuously] cleanse us from all
unrighteousness." 1 John 1:9, The Amplified Bible*

Last year my siblings and I bought our grandparents a new microwave. They desperately needed one. My spunky grandmother had bravely taken on her ancient 1980s toaster oven for far too long. We didn't like the scars she had to prove it. She'd been burned numerous times on the elements that were exposed and had to leave food in far longer than she should to get it to a suitable temperature.

She grinned a huge smile when we walked in with that new machine. She was very grateful and appreciative. She watched intently as my husband unplugged the old one and moved it to make room for the new. We decided to take that huge old clunker down to the local dump to get it out of the way permanently, but my grandmother promptly stopped us when she saw her beloved appliance leaving the house. She asked us to simply put that old one in her basement. She wanted to keep it stored there. We questioned her. Why in the world would she want to keep something old when there was an updated version ready to be used in her kitchen?

"Just in case," she replied.

Are you kidding me? Just in case, what?

God has given His children so many new things to get excited about. His Spirit lives in you, and divine opportunities beckon you to complete your purpose. Along the way you may be tempted to store old habits, preferences, hindrances, and sins *just in case*. Why would you or I hang on to anything old when the new has come (2 Cor. 5:17)? The old might be comfortable, but it's not useful. Today is the day for us to confess and move on.

**Is any old comfort or sin keeping you from yielding to God's divine intervention? If so, why do you think it is hard for you to let it go? Respond in the margin.**

Jonah had a problem letting go. Initially, he'd wanted to keep his own goals and hesitated to fully embrace God's task for him. Now we see a different side of the freshly disciplined prophet. He survived a fierce storm and a brush with death. Now, in the belly of a fish, Jonah thought twice about the things he'd been holding on to and the decisions he'd made. He had decided it was time, once and for all, to come clean and let go.

**Jonah's journey has taught us two things this week. List the two principles we've already covered.**

1. *The blame game – admit our faults, mistakes, sins*

2. *Man overboard – accepting discipline*

The third principle is to "ask for forgiveness." One word encapsulates the essence of this step—*repentance*. Repentance has two aspects:
- Confession means agreeing with God about any sin or rebellion in our lives and asking Him to rid us of that for which we have no more use.
- Change calls for changing our mind, attitude, and actions.

## PRINCIPLE #3—AGREEING WITH GOD

First John 1:9 can be translated: "If we agree with God about our sins, He is faithful and righteous to forgive us our sins and to cleanse us from all unrighteousness." Jonah had come to the point of agreeing with God about his sin. His prayer, in chapter 2, has been likened to the psalms. Its poetry is profound and beautiful. It is filled with all the right words that prove "his theology is as straight as a prophet's should be."[2]

However, whether or not Jonah knew God was never the concern. Clearly he was well acquainted with God. He could discern the leading of God. Yet Jonah had a problem agreeing with God and changing his mind, attitude, and actions to comply with God. His heart was out of alignment with the heart of God. Jesus addressed this issue with the Pharisees.

**Using John 5:39-40, how would you describe to a new believer the difference between knowing about God and agreeing with God?**

*You can be acquainted with God (know about Him) without agreeing with God (& your actions to comply & agree w/His wishes).*

*— We miss the forest for the trees – you can learn about God & bury yourself in the Bible, but He's right in front of you asking for obedience*

67

*"He said, I cried out to the LORD in my great trouble, and he answered me. I called to you from the land of the dead, and LORD, you heard me!"*

*"Then I said, 'O LORD, you have driven me from your presence. Yet <u>I will look once more toward your holy Temple.</u>'"*

*"<u>As my life was slipping away, I remembered the LORD. And my earnest prayer went out to you in your holy Temple.</u>"*

*"But I will offer sacrifices to you with songs of praise, and I will fulfill all my vows. For my salvation comes from the LORD alone."*

Jonah 2:2,4,7,9, NLT

In chapter 1, the sailors on the vessel showed some sort of repentance, and the entire city of Nineveh was about to do the same in chapter 3. Chapter 2 is Jonah's turn. Though he never actually confessed a specific sin, we see he was on the road to repentance because he was willing to make some changes. Even if only because he saw the uselessness in disobedience and was tired of the consequences, Jonah was penitent for the choices he had made and wanted to modify his behavior.

**Read the portions of Jonah 2 in the margin. Underline the phrases that show Jonah's heart beginning to change.**

## TAKING A TURN

Jonah's words not only reveal an agreement with God but also a willingness to act differently. True repentance requires a change in direction. Remember my experience trying to navigate to a new restaurant? To get back on track I couldn't merely admit I was going the wrong way (acknowledge) and be willing to lose ground by backtracking a bit (accept). I had to act—take an exit off the freeway. The longer I waited to exit, the more ground and time I lost. Taking the exit is similar to what it means to repent. It means that we are, by the Spirit's power, willing to stop traveling the direction we've been going.

**Fill in the missing phrase in these three Scriptures.**

**Isaiah 45:22 "** _Turn to Me_ **and be saved, all the ends of the earth; For I am God, and there is no other. "**

**Acts 14:15 "Men, why are you doing these things? We are also men of the same nature as you, and preach the gospel to you that you should** _turn from these worthless things_ **to a living God, WHO MADE THE HEAVEN AND THE EARTH AND THE SEA AND ALL THAT IS IN THEM."**

**1 Thessalonians 1:9 "For they themselves report about us what kind of a reception we had with you, and how you** _turned to God_ **from idols to serve a living and true God."**

**Circle any phrases from Jonah 2 in the margin that show Jonah's desire to turn.**

Remember, Jonah still did not desire to go to Nineveh. We'll find in chapter 4 that he still hoped the Ninevites would not receive God's mercy. This gives us incredible insight into repentance. It doesn't necessarily require that your feelings have changed about what God is asking you to do. Like my grandmother with that outdated appliance, you may very well still have an affinity for the old item in your life.

Repentance means you are willing, despite those feelings, to put it aside and stop traveling the wrong way. The effectiveness of our confession is not negated because of misplaced feelings. Many times God calls us to choose to walk by faith, and our feelings follow along in time.

> **Is God asking you to "exit" in any area of your life?**
> **What specific actions would this require you to make?**

*I don't know what I'm supposed to do*

> **Are you being obedient in some area in spite of your feelings?**

*I'm trying to be obedient & content even though I feel frustrated with my career/financial situation*

## COMPLETELY FORGIVEN

First John 1:9 says that our God is faithful and He will forgive, no matter how far off track you may have gone, how far you may have run, or how much time you may have lost. He's willing to take the old and replace it with the grand newness of life in Him. We don't have to go one more day or even take one more step with the shame of yesterday's choices and unwise decisions weighing us down. He was willing to honor Jonah's desire to yield despite past failure, and He is willing to honor ours as well.

> **Take some time to pray, responding to this portion of Jonah's experience. Ask God to supply you the grace to exit and repent if that's your need or to walk in obedience in spite of the obstacles you face. Like Jonah, you may even need grace to love some Ninevites.**

# COMING CLEAN

*"But I will sacrifice to You with the voice of thanks-*
*giving. That which I have vowed I will pay.*
*Salvation is from the LORD." Jonah 2:9*

One of my favorite television programs is on the Style Network. It's called *Clean House.* During the one-hour program, the zany host and her team tackle the clutter in a person's home. While the handyman builds new shelves to house things strewn across the floors and bed, the decorator begins to sort through what he can use in the new design. The professional organizer sifts mounds of papers and supplies to decide the best way to systematize their items while the yard sale expert cleans the clutter to sell on the front lawn. It's quite an enormous and overwhelming project and is extremely interesting to watch unfold.

During the final minutes of the program, the owners come back to their home to find a completely organized, gorgeously decorated, and squeaky clean home—rid of all the stuff that had weighed it down. Some have laughed in shock, others have cried in grateful wonder, all of them have been stunned to see the unbelievable transformation that has taken place.

The host never leaves before addressing the upkeep of all the work they've done. She invariably explains that her team is leaving and it will be up to the homeowners to choose to live differently than they've done before. No more hoarding. No more laziness. They have to clean, organize, and maintain their home if they want to continue to live in peace.

They have to choose to live differently.

**We've walked through three steps of reconciliation with God. See if you can list them without looking back at your notes.**

1. acknowledge our sin

2. accept God's discipline

3. ask for forgiveness

Our final step—the one that takes all of the resolve that only the Holy Spirit in us can give—is to act in conjunction with God's direction. To cinch the full, wondrous effects of the work He's been doing, you've got to choose to live differently, to walk down a different path, and to maintain what He's put in place.

This week I've been using an illustration of being lost going to a restaurant. Match up each stage of the quest with the stage of reconciliation that it illustrates.

_B_ 1. acknowledge sin

_D_ 2. accept discipline

_A_ 3. ask for forgiveness

_C_ 4. act in conjunction with God's direction

a. take the exit
b. admit I'm headed in the wrong direction
c. find the on-ramp on the other side of the freeway and get back on in the right direction
d. be willing to lose ground I've covered

As best you can determine, to what divine interruption has God called you to surrender right now?

- trust Him totally with my finances
- share His word with others

What are the next steps you can take to get on the "on ramp" and head in the right direction with God?

○ obey the prompting I know I've been receiving from the Holy Spirit

☑ set aside regular time daily to hear God through His Word so I'll know what He's prompting

○ go back and tend to that matter in my past that has been a barrier to hearing God speak

☑ finally break down and surrender to God, turning loose of what I've been grasping

○ get help from a pastor or counselor because this obstacle has proved to be too big for me alone

○ other _____

## PRINCIPLE #4—GOING WITH GOD

"You will pray to Him and He will hear you; and you will pay your vows."
**Job 22:27**

Jonah spent the bulk of his prayer in chapter 2 highlighting the depths to which he had sunk both physically and spiritually. Theologians and scholars debate whether Jonah was alive during those three days in the belly of the fish or whether he died and was brought back to life. In any case, no doubt when he remembered and recorded this prayer long after he had been deposited back onto dry land, he was fully aware that he'd been preserved and protected by Yahweh.

Whether it was the stunning revelation of God's protection or the eye-opening conversation earlier with the sailors during the storm, Jonah decided that being in God's will was the best direction he could travel. He chose to abandon the path of disobedience and defiance and get in step with God's plans.

You may remember that many commentators believe Jonah 2:9 is the heart of the Book of Jonah. In this one verse, Jonah made a firm decision to be obedient to God's directives.

*"But I will sacrifice to You with the voice of thanksgiving. That which I have vowed I will pay. Salvation is from the LORD."*
**Jonah 2:9**

**Consider Jonah 2:9 in the margin. Rewrite the prayer from your personal perspective as if you had prayed it.**

*I will follow your wishes gratefully, and do what I have vowed. Salvation comes from You.*

Jonah did not allow the despair of his circumstances to keep him from firmly agreeing to go with God. While some may have thought they were "too late" to get on board with God's plans or that they'd missed their opportunity, Jonah taught us that any time is a good time to set your sights and actions on obedience.

**Do you struggle with feeling that you have wasted too much time to have another opportunity with God? If so, how does this affect your current actions?**

*Yes, I often feel its "too late" and all my opportunities have passed me by.*

In addition, the prophet's choice of words clues us in to the significance of what it truly means to go where God is leading. Jonah used a Hebrew word translated *vow* in our English Bibles. "In most cases, the context [of this word] shows that the vow implies a promised gift for sacrifice, not merely a course of action as is implied in the English word *vow*."[3] In other words, Jonah was not simply agreeing to go to Nineveh, he was also agreeing to return to the Holy Land to offer the Lord the proper ritual sacrifice in the temple. He wanted to "sacrifice to [God] with the voice of thanksgiving" (2:9). He was referring specifically to the thanksgiving offering that was a holy offering given to the Lord in Jerusalem.

> **From Leviticus 7:12, what were some of the details of the thanksgiving offering?**
>
> *- cakes of bread made w/o yeast, mixed w/oil*
> *- wafers made w/o yeast, spread w/oil*
> *- cakes of flour mixed w/oil*

True sacrificial obedience would cost Jonah something more than just a one-time decision to go to Nineveh. Likewise, we must be willing to obey the small details along the pathway to obedience to the Lord as well.

## LETTING GO

At seminary I attended chapel most every Tuesday. I enjoyed sitting under the powerful teaching of Chuck Swindoll, who was president at the time. One of his stirring illustrations gripped me and has returned to challenge me through the years. He told of a time he'd spoken at a church and had shared a concern he was having with one of his beloved children. After the message an older woman walked up to him as he stood to greet the congregants. As he bent over to hear this tiny woman, she said: "Whatever you are holding on to in this life, hold it loosely so it won't hurt when the Lord has to pry your fingers open to take it away."

Has the divine interruption the Lord has brought your way revealed some things that you are holding on to too tightly? Have you been hurting as He's sought to pry your fingers away from the comfort, ambition, goal, or even the sin that you can barely release?

Jonah's knuckles must have been white with pain as God's holy hand forced his hands open. Flat palmed, he raised his arms to the Lord in sweet surrender and vowed to go with God all the way to Nineveh.

> **End today by literally opening your hands as a symbol of what you are releasing to God. Raise your hands to Him in submission and surrender and commit to go where He is leading.**

*"Offer to God a sacrifice of thanksgiving and pay your vows to the Most High; call upon Me in the day of trouble; I shall rescue you, and you will honor Me."*
**Psalm 50:14-15**

Day 5

# DESPERATE MEASURES

*"I called out of my distress to the Lord and He answered me. I cried for help from the depth of Sheol; You heard my voice." Jonah 2:2*

This week we've done some good work together combing through Jonah 2 and considering the steps of reconciliation with God. We looked at several small portions of this chapter for lessons on recommitting ourselves to the Lord's direction. Jonah 2 also contains some valuable themes that can enhance our prayer lives. Let's conclude our week by looking at three major themes related to prayer: the pattern of prayer, the passion of prayer, and the posture of prayer.

## A LESSON IN REPEATING

Jonah must have known Scripture, in particular the psalms. Much of chapter 2 seems to mirror the words written by the psalmists. Since Jonah didn't have a pad and paper—much less a scroll of the Old Testament with him in the fish that day, he had an arsenal of memorized verses freshly stamped on his heart and mind. When he prayed from the belly of the fish, Jonah didn't utter much that was original and innovative. Rather he repeated some of what had already been recorded. Instead of working from scratch, he followed the pattern outlined in the Book of Psalms.

**Choose three of the following pairs of verses and note the corresponding terminology or thoughts:**

Jonah 2:2—Psalm 30:3 — *"I called" for help from "the pit" "the depths" & you heard me / healed me*

*"deep calls to deep"* Jonah 2:3— Psalm 42:7

Jonah 2:5—Psalm 69:1-2 *engulfed, drowning in deep waters*

Jonah 2:7—Psalm 18:6

Jonah 2:9—Psalm 66:13-14 *I will fulfill / make good my vows to You*

Jonah 2 shows the power of praying the Scriptures. His words appear as a tapestry of psalms knitted together to form his personal prayer for his unique situation. In dire circumstances the disciplined preacher didn't waste a moment uttering his own words or wishes. His mind went straight to God's Word and repeated it out loud.

Friend, no prayer is more effective than the one that finds its roots in the pages of God's Word. Jonah challenges us: Have we taken time to inscribe God's Word on our hearts so we have a framework of verses to construct our prayer in the time of need?

## A LESSON IN CRYING

Jude, my one year old, knows how to get my attention. When his brothers take away something he wants or he isn't getting his sippy cup quickly enough, he knows a good zealous cry will bring me to his aid. While he still doesn't always get what he was after, he does garner my attention.

The second thing Jonah's prayer teaches about effective prayer is passionate prayer. Verse 2 suggests Jonah's words weren't uttered in a soft monotone but rang out with fervor. I suspect they were stopped only as they echoed off the walls of the fish's belly. He "cried out." The Hebrew word implies intensity of action that was reserved only for the most heartfelt prayers. This word is only used 22 times in the Bible and the majority of those times it is used autobiographically—as Jonah used it—to denote one who recognizes his own prayer as fervent and records: "I cried."[4]

While fervent prayers do not always guarantee an affirmative answer from God, they do seem to capture His attention in a powerful way. Look at the Scriptures below and answer the questions.

| Exodus 2:23-25 | 2 Samuel 22:1,4-7 |
|---|---|
| **Who is the passage about?** | |
| The Israelites | The Lord (David's song of praise to Him) |
| **What words denote that they prayed with passion?** | |
| "they groaned" & "cried out" for help | "In my distress I called" "my cry" |
| **What was their dilemma?** | |
| They were enslaved | David was pursued by Saul |
| **What was God's response?** | |
| He heard their call, remembered His covenant w/ Abraham, & was concerned about them | God heard his voice (call) & he was saved from his enemies |

**Describe the last time you prayed fervently, passionately, or intensely. What was it about?**

*Today (every day) - I have been praying for help+ praying for discernment to know what TART (Action) I should do About my finances, & for help to trust God completely about it)*

Raising our voices in prayer matters less than engaging our hearts in the passionate pursuit of Him. Prayer easily becomes a rote exercise on which we place little importance and in which we invest less effort. Jonah's story teaches us that the desperate circumstances we find ourselves in while navigating a life interrupted require desperate measures, not the least of which is a revamping of our prayer lives from meaningless words to carefully calculated dialogue. Purposeful prayer must engage our mind, will, and emotion.

## A LESSON IN GRATITUDE

*"In everything give thanks; for this is God's will for you in Christ Jesus."*
1 Thessalonians 5:18

Jonah's prayer is not for deliverance; it is a prayer of deliverance.

The words I most remember from my gymnastics coach: "posture is everything." As a tall preteen trying to overcompensate for my long, gangly legs and uncoordinated torso, she'd often come behind me and shove her palm into the small of my back while pulling back on my shoulders.

"Priscilla, it's all in the way you stand."

The third overarching lesson we learn from Jonah is the posture of prayer. Jonah was in a desperate situation and yet his prayer was not *for* deliverance. It was a prayer *of* deliverance. He was expressing his gratitude to God for the preservation and protection He had already graciously allowed the wayward prophet. Even in the midst of a situation still marked by peril and danger, Jonah prayed with thanksgiving. His vow to the Lord was a promise to praise Him even though he did not know how the Lord would allow the circumstance to work itself out.

Yesterday we noted that should the Lord allow, Jonah purposed to go back to the Holy City to participate in the thanksgiving offering, which included animal sacrifice and cereal offering. But he did more than offer to do it. He offered to do it in a particular posture—"with a voice of thanksgiving." This has at its root the Hebrew word *todah*. "The sense here appears to be songs accompanying the making of a sacrifice."[5] Jonah not only intended to give actual sacrifices but also verbal ones—the sacrifice of praise.

While you and I, under the New Covenant, are not involved with the ceremonies and sacrifices of the Old Testament temple, there is still a sacrifice that we can give.

Describe "the sacrifice of praise" as outlined in Hebrews 13:15 in the margin.

*Give thanks (confess) to His Name*

*"Through Him then, let us continually offer up a sacrifice of praise to God, that is, the fruit of lips that give thanks to His name."*
Hebrews 13:15

Read Habakkuk 3:17-18. What made praise sacrificial in this instance? *Being joyful in God even though we have not seen an answer to our prayer yet (deliverance)*

What would "sacrificial praise" look like in your life today? What would make it a sacrifice?

*Being thankful for what I have & rejoice in the Lord even though I am still in the midst of financial difficulty*

## IN JESUS' NAME, AMEN

Jonah's prayer was deliberate from the very first word to the very last. This is what desperate measures require. Even in his final statement, he uttered, "Deliverance is from the Lord" (NRSV). The Hebrew word used for deliverance is a derivative of the name *Yesuah*. This was the name Mary would be told centuries later that she was to give her son. "The Christian reader who hears this conclusion to Jonah's prayer in its original language cannot miss this word that sounds so much like the Hebrew name of Jesus, which has meant deliverance and salvation for the peoples of the world."[6] What a fitting way for Jonah to conclude his prayer—with a reminder that true deliverance and salvation can only come from Yesuah, the One true Savior and Lord.

Conclude today's lesson by choosing two verses, one from each column. Combine them in your own words to write a prayer to God. Then verbalize this prayer with passion to the Lord.

| THANKSGIVING | DISTRESS |
|---|---|
| 2 Samuel 22:50 | Job 30:16 |
| Psalm 97:12 | Psalm 25:18 |

*I rejoice in the Lord, & I praise Your holy name!*

- *Suffering grips me*
- *Look upon my distress & take away all my sins*

**Note this week's navigation tools.**

Day 1 *ask God for Guidance & Admit when were off course & Accept discipline*

Day 2 *Accept discipline*

Day 3 *Get in agreement w/ God's plan*

Day 4 *Let go of things that prevent us from following God*

Day 5 *Pray w/ Passion & power of Scripture*

*Even though suffering grips me I rejoice in You, Lord, and all your blessings. Please look upon my financial distress, & take away all my sins. I pray this in Your name & praise Your Name—*

# Session 4
## VIEWER GUIDE

The _Rhema_ word is God's specific word to you.

*"Now the word of the LORD came to Jonah the second time"* (Jonah 3:1).
God gives us a second chance (opportunity)

_Forgiveness_ of past sin qualifies us for present service.

*"I permitted Myself to be sought by those who did not ask for Me; I permitted Myself to be found by those who did not seek Me. I said, 'Here am I, here am I,' to a nation which did not call on My name. I have spread out My hands all day long to a rebellious people, who walk in the way which is not good, following their own thoughts, a people who continually provoke Me to My face"* (Isa. 65:1-3).

*"Arise, go to Nineveh the great city and proclaim to it the proclamation which I am going to tell you"* (Jonah 3:2).

God has put Himself in you to _equip_ you and _empower_ you to do what you cannot do.

You get a _second chance_.

*"Arise, go to Nineveh the great city and proclaim to it the proclamation which I am going to tell you"* (Jonah 3:2). God is w/ you along the way empowering & Instructing you along the new path

**You get the** <u>presence</u> **of** <u>God</u>.
(To help you do what you can't do on your own)

(at the moment of your salvation)

**Once <u>you receive the Holy Spirit</u> and He is in you, He can't be taken away.**

*"Even if our gospel is veiled, it is veiled to those who are perishing, in whose case the god of this world has blinded the minds of the unbelieving so that they might not see the light of the gospel of the glory of Christ, who is the image of God"* (2 Cor. 4:3-4).

*"So Jonah arose and went to Nineveh according to the word of the LORD. Now Nineveh was an exceedingly great city, a three days' walk"* (Jonah 3:3).

**It is easy for us to** <u>impersonate</u> **obedience.**
(we outwardly look obedient, but our heart isn't in it)

# Second Chances

# Take Two

*"Now the word of the Lord came to Jonah the second time, saying, arise, go to Nineveh." Jonah 3:1-2*

The most humbling times in my life are undoubtedly when I am on a platform teaching God's people. With Bible perched under my arm, notes tucked inside, heart palpitating in my chest, and eyes scanning the crowd, I ask the audience to bow for a quick prayer before the message begins. I'm praying not only because I need God's empowerment but because I need a minute to gain my composure.

You see, I'm stunned. Every time I'm getting ready to open God's Word and teach from it, I'm in complete disbelief. Why He didn't relegate me to the proverbial shelf long ago, I'll never know. Like Jonah, in so many moments of rebellion, I've chosen a lifestyle out of sync with God's will for me. Yet for some odd reason He lets me partner with Him.

I handle this position with care. I'm too shocked to do otherwise.

Aren't you? Isn't there something God has allowed in your life, some type of beauty-for-ashes miracle He has allowed, the sight of which causes you to simply stand back, mouth agape in wonder, and stare?

How can we not take time to relish the wonder of God's mercy? Today is our chance to celebrate the mystery of divine second chances.

Jonah 3 is such a triumphant celebration of return and restoration. It is a stunning and fantastic reminder of the mercy and grace available to all those who have messed up and need to know that they aren't all washed up. Let's look at a few memorable "second-chance" miracles from Scripture and then consider them in light of our own lives.

## CELEBRATION OF SECOND CHANCES
### Aaron

Aaron is known mostly as Moses' brother. He played second fiddle to Moses, serving as his mouthpiece when he went to stand before Pharaoh. In the wilderness, when the Israelites waged war against the Amalekites, Aaron wasn't in the trenches of battle but stood beside his brother, holding up his hands in prayer. Aaron seemed to have a hard time coming out from underneath the shadow of his younger brother. Yet he had a high calling on his life by God as well.

To what position was Aaron being called (Ex. 28:1-3)?

*To serve as priest*

Have you ever lived under another's shadow and wondered if God had a significant call on your life? ⊘ yes ○ no  If so, how did you feel and how did you handle the situation?

*I still feel that way - I still feel like everyone else has their time in the sun & I'm still waiting*

God set Aaron aside to officiate in the tabernacle. As the high priest, he served as the mediator between God and His chosen people. He had the privilege of entering the most holy place and experiencing the delight of God's presence in a way few ever would. Aaron's garments were specifically prepared to distinguish him and ascribed dignity to his role within the community of faith.

While Moses was on Mount Sinai (Ex. 28) receiving instructions from God for the making of Aaron's garment and his consecration, things began to unravel. At this moment of divine dialogue between Moses and Yahweh, a great injustice was occurring at the foot of the mountain.

Turn to Exodus 32:1-5. What were the people doing?

*They made a golden idol to worship, sacrificed burnt offerings & indulged in revelry*

Who was organizing their activities?

*Aaron*

Can you imagine Moses' disbelief at Aaron's actions when he stepped foot off Sinai? While Moses may have been shocked, God was not. Even while He was giving instructions to Moses, God was fully aware of His chosen vessel staging a rebellion against Him. Yet Aaron was given a second chance. He was still allowed to serve as Israel's first high priest.

I want you to take time now to carefully consider Aaron's story in light of your own. Be as thoughtful and as detailed as you possibly can. Have you ever seen in hindsight the work God was doing on your behalf—the second chance He was preparing for you—even while you were in a season of sin?

How does this affect your appreciation of Him and what He's given you?

*He has always given me "second chances" after I've made stupid decisions (career, finances, marriage), and it deepens my appreciation of Him and the blessings I have now*

## Sarah

Sarah was Abraham's wife. God gave her a promise; she would have a son and become mother of an entire nation of people. Abraham and Sarah had a track record of trusting God. When God told him to leave Ur and go to an unspecified place, they did it with no questions asked. But when God said she'd be pregnant, she'd gotten a hearty laugh out of it considering her age and infertility. Ultimately, she knew that neither were hurdles too big for God to overcome, but after 10 years of waiting to see proof of God's promise, Sarah's resolve began to wane.

*"For the vision is yet for the appointed time; it hastens toward the goal and it will not fail. Though it tarries, wait for it; for it will certainly come, it will not delay."*
**Habakkuk 2:3**

**What did Sarah do about the situation in Genesis 16:3?**

*She gave her maidservant Hagar to Abraham to be his wife, so a child would be conceived by them*

I must admit, I can relate to Sarah's desire to help God get a move on. Sometimes His timetable is a bit hard to rest in, isn't it? I wish I were better in the area of patience, but it's one of the aspects of the fruit of God's Spirit I need to take a few more bites of.

**Do you normally have trouble waiting for God to make good on His Word? How does this show up in your life?**

*Yes! Feelings of impatience*

Sarah's choice and Abraham's compliance resulted in an illegitimate child named Ishmael. He was not the seed through which the chosen nation would come. While Abraham begged God to use Ishmael, God held His ground and told Abraham that though He would bless Ishmael and give him many descendents, Sarah would still bear a child and he would be the son of promise. (See Gen. 17:17-21.)

**How was Sarah given a second chance (Gen. 17:21)?**

*She conceived Isaac, who was the chosen son*

**How do Sarah's actions and her second chance mirror your life? When have you sought to "help God" by moving ahead of Him when you became impatient?**

*Jumping at the wrong opportunities*

## Peter

A Galilean fisherman and among the first called to be a disciple, Peter quickly emerged as a leader among the Twelve. As a part of his calling,

Peter received a name that means *rock*. He was strong, assertive, and memorable. Always mentioned first in lists of the Twelve and singled out for special revelations of Jesus' deity, Peter pledged to follow Jesus to the death. So the Messiah's prophecy that Peter would soon deny their relationship three times seemed hard to believe. But Peter soon did just that.

> **After denying Christ in Matthew 26:69-75, what caused Peter to recall Jesus' prophecy? How did he respond?**

*a Rooster crowing, as Jesus prophesied. He went outside & wept*

After such a fall it seemed Peter's job as a disciple was over. What employer would ever keep a staff member who was disloyal and untrustworthy— much less offer him a promotion within the organization? Certainly he'd not be allowed to have a close intimate relationship with the One he'd just so vehemently denied. Yet a close look at a tender conversation between the resurrected Jesus and the disreputable disciple tells us otherwise.

> **What three ministry directives did Jesus give Peter? Read John 21:15-17.**

*Feed my lambs, Take care of my sheep, Feed my sheep.*

> **How is your story like Peter's? In the margin describe a time when you thought you'd never be used by God again, but you were.**

*I still feel like I'm waiting to know how God wants to use me in the first place.*

## THANK GOD FOR A SECOND CHANCE

Jonah's heart must have been filled with gratitude. While he was still not thrilled about going to Nineveh, he couldn't believe God would ever use him again in any sort of assignment. He had chosen to run away in rebellion, yet God still singled him out to be the first Israelite to take the message of Yahweh's mercy to pagans. What a high calling! What a great opportunity! What an immense privilege! Jonah was the first missionary— the reluctant missionary.

Aaron, Sarah, Peter, and Jonah were given a gift still available to you and me as well. Have you fallen out of fellowship with God? Have you made decisions that have taken you further down a path of rebellion than you ever thought you'd go? You've not outrun the grasp of His grace or overstepped the boundaries of His mercy. It is still available for you—for me—right here and right away.

Thank God for a second chance.

Day 2

# THE CELEBRATION CONTINUES

*"He kissed all his brothers." Genesis 45:15*

At the end of yesterday's lesson, I had trouble peeling myself away from my keyboard. I could have written for hours. I was overwhelmed by all the second-chance stories in Scripture. The Bible bulges with account after merciful account of individuals who'd blown it and yet were offered the clemency that only a compassionate God like ours could give.

So let the celebration carry on!

I hope that you will continue to see bits of your story and glimpses of His grace as you examine more of these riveting narratives.

## JOSEPH'S BROTHERS

Joseph's 10 brothers appear in the Book of Genesis as a jealous and conniving brood who were out to seek revenge on their younger brother. They were tired of living in the shadow of the son born to their father's favored wife. Joseph seemed to enjoy a preferential status highlighted by a brilliant robe. Envy roared out of control and burst into flames of violence. They plotted to kill their brother, but plans changed when some passing merchants agreed to buy Joseph as a slave.

**Have you ever been betrayed by a friend or family member?** ⊘ yes ◯ no **If so, list three words to describe your feelings about the incident.**

*yes, by my parents — Angry, hurt, mistrustful of them*

**Have you ever betrayed a friend or family member?** ◯ yes ⊘ no **If so, list three words to describe your feelings about it at the time.**

Genesis 39–41 chronicles a sorrowful tale. The merchants who purchased Joseph sold him in Egypt. Can you imagine the despondency and heartache that must have ripped through his young heart each night? Yet "the

LORD was with Joseph" (Gen. 39:2), and despite the circumstances he had already faced and would face in the future, he rose to prominence and success within the ranks of the Egyptian nation. Pretty soon he was a trusted overseer in the home of a high-ranking official.

**In the margin record some details about a time when you saw God inexplicably bring positive results out of negative beginnings.** *Russ & Margie*

When a famine struck, Joseph "administers the grain reserves for the benefit of the Egyptians, and, indeed for all the people of the world."[1] This famine proved the catalyst to bring us to the story's climax. For Joseph's brothers were forced to flee to Egypt in search of food. They came face-to-face with Joseph and were at his mercy. While he was completely aware of their identity, they didn't know him until he chose to reveal himself.

**Read the account of Joseph's revelation (Gen. 45:1-8). What was Joseph's emotional state when he revealed himself to his brothers?**

*Weeping*

**What was the brothers' emotional state?**

*Terrified of what Joseph might do to them*

**Whom did Joseph tell the brothers was responsible for his being sold into slavery?**

*God (sending him ahead to save lives)*

**What did he say was the purpose for his being sold into slavery?**

*To save lives*

**When you have been betrayed by another, were you able to see God's hand in the situation? If so, how?**

*not Really*

Joseph could have had his brothers killed or severely punished for the injustice done to him, but in a breathtaking act of mercy, he "kissed all his brothers" and invited them to live under his provision and protection. In a true picture of the merciful Savior to come, Joseph refrained from anger, abstained from vengeance, and offered that which was not deserved.

When you have been the betrayer, how have the actions of the person you offended been like or unlike Jesus Christ?

What did their actions teach you about the Lord's love?

Put yourself in the story. How can you relate to Joseph's brothers? How has Jesus been like Joseph to you?

*If I were in their shoes, I would have been just as terrified of Joseph. Jesus has always given me more chances and new opportunities*

## SHEEP, COINS, AND SONS

What do a sheep, a coin, and a son all have in common? Absolutely nothing unless they are woven into a divine tale straight from the lips of Jesus. While the story of the prodigal son is more familiar, the others are shorter and often overlooked. Let's concentrate on these two.

Only in one place in Scripture did Jesus tell three parables to make one point. In Luke 15, He was surrounded by the city's scoundrels and its elite. Sinners flanked Him on one side and the Pharisees and scribes on the other. It must have been quite a scene that day as the riffraff pressed in to hear Jesus and the Jewish leaders pressed in to criticize Him.

The religious leaders couldn't believe Jesus would allow such people to get so close. The Messiah must have overheard their grumblings because He promptly told them about a sheep, a coin, and a son that all had one thing in common: They were lost and then joyfully rediscovered.

### Lost Because of Foolishness

Jesus wanted everyone to relate, so He started in on the men and the boys first with a tale of a beloved sheep who strayed. Sheep have a propensity to wander. Any shepherd worth his salt had to work overtime to keep his precious flock in check. Yet there always seemed to be one that slipped his careful watch and steered off the beaten path. What great concern must have been in the shepherd's heart to cause him to leave his others behind in search of just that one. While they were equally as important, they were safely in his care. So he went looking for the foolish one that didn't even know the danger it was in.

In hindsight, can you now see a dangerous place you put yourself in because of foolishness? What blinded you at the time to the danger?

What made the shepherd's actions so gracious?

*He showed mercy*

## Lost Because of Carelessness

If the Jewish leaders wanted to hurl a retort for the tale of the sheep, they'd have to wait. No sooner had Jesus concluded His story about the retrieval of the lost sheep than He was on to a story about a coin.

No doubt, the women in the group leaned forward in anticipation. "When a Jewish girl married, she began to wear a headband of ten silver coins to signify that she was now a wife. It was the Jewish version of our modern wedding ring, and it would be considered a calamity for her to lose one of those coins."[2] Jesus told of a woman who had a band with one lost coin. He asked the crowd to consider how a woman in this position would address the situation. Would she just sit back and hope that it turned up on its own? Certainly not! She began an all-out search-and-rescue adventure.

I rarely take off my wedding ring, but on one occasion I did and my young son got hold of it. There was no piece of furniture, rug, or appliance left unturned until it was safely back where it belonged. Sheer panic melted into sweet relief the moment it was back on my finger.

What difference do you see between how the sheep and the coin were lost?

*The sheep were lost through their own action (wandering off)*

How have you seen the Lord work diligently to "find" you on the occasions when you've suffered consequences for carelessness?

The message of these parables were revolutionary to the first century Jewish mind. Never had they considered that God would search for the lost. They didn't think He cared that much or that He would expend that much energy on one lost soul. They thought it was man's job to seek God and, if anything, God was doing the hiding. While these parables certainly speak to those in need of salvation, their message unveils the heart of our servant Savior to seek out, save, and salvage those He loves.

> Historically, have you seen God more as someone searching you out and eagerly awaiting an opportunity to give you a second chance or hiding from you?

*Mostly as someone eagerly awaiting for relationship with me (and all of us) & to show us mercy. When God seems to be "hiding" I know He's still working behind the scenes*

> What teachings or experiences have helped to shape your view in this regard? Prepare to discuss this with your group.

*Opportunities or new chances have appeared when I needed them the most. (New job offer, Mom's home selling)*

> Record the parallel conclusion in the case of the sheep, the coin, and the son from Luke 15:6,9,22-24.

*they were all found*

For two days we've had a celebration of second chances. Now consider the fact that God is having one too! If you've chosen to abandon the pathway of rebellion and yield to the divine interruption God is allowing, then know that your Savior is celebrating. And I assure you, you've never been to a bash that was bigger, better, or more extravagant than this one.

Yesterday and today we've seen that the ancient biblical record gives us modern-day encouragement. Your "second chance" story could be a great encouragement to others who may question God's grace in the future.

On a separate sheet of paper use the remainder of your time to summarize the details of one or more of your second chance stories into bullet points that will help you to share with your group this week. Then prioritize the points, taking time to write a letter sharing your story. Put it in a place where it can be preserved and kept for years to come to remind your children and grandchildren that they too serve a God of second chances.

# SHORTCUTS

*"Then the LORD commanded the fish, and it vomited
Jonah onto the dry land." Jonah 2:10*

I'm not the most technologically savvy person in the world, but I have
become very adept at texting. In a few seconds, using the tip of my right
thumb, I can hash out a message complete with jokes and appropriate
slang. I've gotten pretty skillful at the little shortcuts that make words
easier to manage and quicker to type. With only 140 characters per Twit-
tering message, I've become masterful at finding short ways to say things.

My fondness for shortening words seeps over into writing. Sometimes
sitting at my laptop, books and commentaries strewn around me and writing
project before me, I'll hurriedly type "Lol" instead of explaining how funny
something was or type "2" instead of writing out the number. I've had to
erase, rewrite, and remind myself that shortcuts aren't always best.

After second-chance celebrations, today's subject might be a startling
brush with reality—no shortcuts with God. Our second chance brings us
full circle to the place where we have to choose full obedience. While we may
want to find the easiest road to complete obedience, our heart must be set
on doing God's will—His way and in its entirety—even if it takes longer than
we'd prefer or requires more effort.

**What were God's instructions to Jonah in Jonah 3:2?**

*Go to Ninevah & proclaim the message God gave him*

**To which verse in chapter 1 does this relate?** *Verse 2*

Jonah had been disciplined and decided to get on board with God's plan.
At the appropriate time, God commanded the fish to release the prophet.
Scripture does not say where the fish deposited Jonah, but "it is reasonable
to assume that Jonah was right back near Joppa where he started."[3]

Not only must Jonah have been amazed to still be alive, but he must
have been startled when he got his bearings and realized that he was back
at square one with the same command he'd fled before. For him, there'd be
no getting out of God's will, no shortcut to Nineveh. He hadn't gotten a full
ride to the shores of Assyria courtesy of the "Big Fish Express." Full detailed
obedience would be required.

Have you ever tried to circumvent God's instructions or do them halfway? What did this look like in your life?

## DETAILED DELIVERANCE

Lots of scriptural examples show people who tried to take a shortcut when it came to obeying God. Abraham had an illicit relationship that yielded Ishmael instead of waiting on God's timing and promise. Saul kept some of the best spoils of the Amalekites instead of destroying everything as God instructed him. In Matthew 19 the rich young man wanted to achieve salvation by doing everything but what Jesus required. In fact, it seems even Satan knows the unbelievably tragic effects taking shortcuts can have because he even tried to get Jesus to take the easy road (Matt. 4).

In 2 Kings we meet Naaman, a man who learned an important lesson about the details of obedience. He was captain of the Syrian army and highly respected for the battles he'd waged and won. You'd think a man in charge of a vast army would appreciate the gravity of meticulously receiving and following instructions, yet he was unwilling to do so himself.

Naaman had leprosy. When he learned that a prophet in Samaria might be able to heal him, he got a letter from his king to take to the king of Israel requesting his help in the matter. While the request for healing overwhelmed the king of Israel, Elisha was determined to show Naaman that there was a prophet in Israel (2 Kings 5:8) and that the God of Israel could heal. Naaman came to Elisha and received specific instructions.

What mandate did Elisha give Naaman in 2 Kings 5:10-11?

*Wash yourself 7 times in the Jordan*

What was Naaman's response?

*He went away angry ~ he had expected more*

If you had been Naaman, how would you have responded to Elisha's instructions?
- ○ I'd be mad because they seemed ridiculous.
- ○ I'd be embarrassed to carry them out.
- ⊘ I'd think they were too simple to achieve anything.
- ○ I wouldn't take time to think. I'd just obey.

Naaman had several problems with Elisha's instructions. He didn't like what he was told to do, how Elisha told him to do it, or where he was told to carry out the instructions. Naaman's preconceived ideas of how his healing would take place initially kept him from humbly doing what God required. He even suggested a better method to procure his healing (v. 12).

What does Naaman's suggestion of a different process imply that he felt …

about the prophet

about God

> *He didn't believe or trust their solution*

about himself  *He knew better than the prophet & God*

The waters of Abanah and Pharpar were in Naaman's hometown. He knew them to be clean and clear waters compared to the Jordan. He was appalled that someone of his stature would have to dip himself into such dirty waters. The Syrian rivers would not only be cleaner but more convenient. He didn't think the Jordan River could possibly do him any good.

Prayerfully consider the following questions regarding your current divine interruption. Are you having more trouble with:
○ what God has asked you to do
○ how God has asked you to do it
○ where God has asked you to do it

*I don't know what I'm supposed to do except trust God*

In the margin explain which of these, if any, has kept you from moving forward in obedience to God. *Fear, worry about finances*

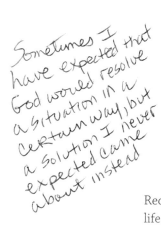
*Sometimes I have expected that God would resolve a situation in a certain way, but a solution I never expected came about instead*

Have you made suggestions to God about what might be a "better" way to accomplish the task at hand?

What does this say about the way you feel about God, yourself, or His Word?  *The human part of me is still not fully trusting God in this*

Recently at a church in Maryland, I spoke on Jonah and the interrupted life. Afterward, an older woman walked up to me with a solemn facial expression. She seemed overwhelmed and frustrated as she began, "Thanks for your message. I needed to hear it. I raised three children and was looking forward to retirement. I've yet to enjoy it because my daughter has made some bad choices and I am now raising my four grandchildren. I know it's the right thing and I love them dearly, but I'm often tempted to find another place for them to grow up. I'm a bit frustrated at what God has asked of me for this season of life. It's not what I had in mind."

While I encouraged this sweet grandmother as best I could that day, I understood her concern and could relate to her temptation. This is precisely the way we feel when, like Naaman and this godly woman in Maryland, we meet up with instructions from God that don't fit with what we had in mind or seem to be unnecessarily inopportune.

Our inclination would be to find another route to accomplish what God requires that won't take as much effort or energy as we will have to expend to obey God completely. Yet Joppa—the place of decision and the crossroads of obedience—seems to be the starting place of most second chances.

**In the margin write about what represents Joppa in your situation. Be as detailed as you can. What are the original instructions and circumstances that represent your place of decision?** *Trust God completely with my finances (including donating to Eastpoint's relocation plan)*

Naaman's wise servants, people who knew the value of carrying out instructions with precision, encouraged him and eventually caused him to see the futility of trying to circumvent God's directions. What Naaman needed to learn is the same thing we do: full obedience to the Word of God makes the difference.

The work God is trying to do in you requires your full participation. You will find the rewards when you subscribe completely to what He asks and do the tasks how and where He asks.

**What do you see about this principle in Jesus' example from John 4:34 and Philippians 2:8?**

*He knew His work was to do God's will & accomplish His mission, obedient to the point of death*

Jonah was back at Joppa and had to devote himself fully to God's will. No shortcuts could navigate the 500 miles to Nineveh. He had to put one foot in front of the other and trust God for the rest. Now it was time to obey fully, completely, wholeheartedly.

Today consider if you are trying to take any shortcuts to get out of the full responsibility of God's will for you right now.

*"Jesus said to them, 'My food is to do the will of Him who sent Me and to accomplish His work.'"*
**John 4:34**

*"Being found in appearance as a man, He humbled Himself by becoming obedient to the point of death, even death on a cross."*
**Philippians 2:8**

# MOVING FORWARD

*"I delight to do Your will, O my God;*
*Your law is within my heart." Psalm 40:8*

Last evening was a long one. What was supposed to be a fun day of after school outside playtime followed by a family picnic dinner turned sour when I got news that one of my sons had been disobedient to his teacher at school. His teacher sent me messages letting me know about a stubborn rebellious streak rearing its ugly head. While I have a tiny inkling about where it came from, the behaviors he'd exhibited were unacceptable.

So instead of a festive family afternoon, I had to split my time between the two who wanted to continue with our plans and the one who was relegated to the house. There he sat, pouting at the kitchen table. I took out his homework folder and noticed that he had more work in it than normal. Instead of the usual few math or spelling worksheets, he had accumulated quite a stack. A note from the teacher explained: "I'm sorry that there is more work than normal. This is not only your son's homework but also the work he refused to do in class today. Thank you for your help."

When I put the familiar worksheets in front of him, he squirmed at the sight. Seemed like déjà vu and it was, and then some.

At first glance Jonah's instructions may appear exactly the same. Indeed, he may have felt a mild case of déjà vu. Yet a closer examination of the second round of instructions reveals a bit more on the table than before.

**Yesterday you looked briefly at Jonah 1:2 and 3:2. Today take more time to compare and contrast the details of these verses. Record what the prophet was told to do in Nineveh in each instance.**

1:2 *Go to Nineveh & preach against it.*

3:2 *Go to Nineveh & proclaim to it the message I give you*

**What would have been your main concern if you'd received the instructions in 3:2?**

*What exactly is the message to be proclaimed?*

While the destination of Jonah's mission was the same, the directives slightly changed. In chapter 1, his instructions were clearer. God implicitly told Jonah what to do on Assyrian soil. Both His message and its purpose were unmistakable.

On receiving a second chance, Jonah still knew it would require a one-way ticket out of town. He was still aware that a proclamation must be made, but he had received ambiguous insight on what that message should be. So now, instead of simply being required to go, he had to move forward without preassembled plans and details. While both commands required obedience, this one necessitated a greater measure of faith.

**What does Jonah's willingness to yield to this second command reveal about the transformation in his heart?**

*His heart is now willing to be obedient*

**How do you normally respond when God asks you to do something but doesn't reveal the details?**
- ☑ take the first step believing He'll reveal the rest in time
- ○ beg Him to reveal the entire plan first
- ☑ move forward but only timidly
- ○ stay put

**What impact has this choice made in your life? Respond in the margin.** *It has usually worked out*

## STEP BY STEP

One of my favorite passages in all of Scripture is John 16. In this chapter, Jesus spoke tenderly with the disciples on the eve of His crucifixion. They were sorrowful because He had explained in no uncertain terms that He would soon be leaving them and returning to the Father. In an effort to calm their emotions, He explained that it was advantageous to them for Him to leave. He described a coming Holy Spirit whose job it would be to help them, convict them, and guide them.

**Why do you think Jesus told the disciples it was better for Him to leave and the Spirit to come (John 16:7)?**

*Because the Spirit will convict people of sin & guilt*

**Missionary Assignment**

Contemplate the ways you are clear and the ways you are unclear about how to reach the Ninevites the Lord is sending your group to. As a group, spend time in prayer asking for continued clarity on how to serve them.

**What advantages do you see in Jesus' leaving them? How have you seen this evident in your own life?**

*Because only then can the Holy Spirit come*

Can you imagine the intrigue in this moment? The Twelve must have listened intently. Each statement Jesus spoke must have dripped with fascination as He described the Spirit who would indwell them. In the midst of spilling all the juicy details, Jesus stopped and said: "I have many more things to say to you, but you cannot bear them now" (John 16:12).

Have you had a friend do this to you? Lead you to the tip of a conversational cliff only to leave you hanging? Frustrating. Plain ole frustrating.

While talking on the phone to my friend yesterday, I was completely immersed in the conversation. Unaware of the time that was passing or the demands I was avoiding, I sat, totally engrossed and hanging on every word. That's when she did it. She cut me loose. Hung me out to dry.

"Girl, I'll tell you the rest tomorrow. I gotta go."

What? You can't do this to me!

**Contemplate your divine intervention. Make a thoughtful and thorough list of the details you'd like to know that God has yet to give you.**

*—What am I supposed to do career-wise*
*— Am I supposed to stay in this home or sell it?*
*— Am I supposed to stay in Maine?*

**What are your feelings about not knowing?**
- ⊘ frustrated
- ⊘ scared
- ⊘ paralyzed
- ⊘ nervous
- ⊘ overwhelmed
- ○ other

*"No longer do I call you slaves, for the slave does not know what his master is doing; but I have called you friends, for all things that I have heard from My Father I have made known to you."*
**John 15:15**

Jesus knows a thing or two about timing and almost always operates on a step-by-step plan with His children. Just as He determined the disciples had received their full share of information on the occasion in John 16, He is also well aware of when you and I have reached our capacity for hearing and understanding His plans. While our insatiable desire to know it all seems to rarely be satisfied, we must discipline ourselves to place confidence in His decision to give us the information we need to successfully accomplish the step we are on in the journey. He doesn't withhold information because He doesn't love you but because of His great love for you.

# GOOD GUIDANCE

When Jerry and I were first married and didn't have a brood of boys, we traveled to the Holy Land. We had the most wonderful and knowledgeable tour guide. I was amazed by his explanation at each location. I had my notebook and pen in hand and took a prodigious amount of notes.

At the end of our 10-day excursion, I thought back over all the places we'd been, glanced at my notes, and was overwhelmed. I realized then the importance of only receiving information a bit at a time.

If our guide had looked us in the eyes on day one, given us a map with the major places circled, a rundown of each location's significance, and then sent us on our way, it would have been a catastrophe. It would have been far too much for us to absorb and would have resulted in confusion yielding a horrible tour. Our amazing trip came as a direct result of following him from one destination to the next, leaning in and listening to each explanation, and engaging in his wisdom step-by-step. This is what good guidance looks like.

**Answer the following based on John 16:13-14:**

**Who did Jesus promise was coming?**

*The Spirit of truth*

**What would His primary role be?**

*To guide / tell what is yet to come*

**From where would His messages come?**

*Jesus*

**Look back at your notes from this week's video session. How does the promise in John 14:26 relate to Jonah 3:2?**

*Both promise a message (teaching) to be revealed*

> *"The Helper, the Holy Spirit, whom the Father will send in My name, He will teach you all things, and bring to your remembrance all that I said to you."*
> **John 14:26**

God gave the Spirit to the disciples as an internal compass to help them find their way. They could rest easy in Jesus' departure and the partial information He'd given them not because they had enough notes from their three years with Him to carry them the rest of the way but because a wise and wonderful Director would be with them to give them step-by-step instructions. If they'd listen, He'd guide. If they'd follow, He'd lead. The result—a life well lived and a journey well taken.

This week you've explored your second chance. I hope you've committed yourself to complete and full obedience. Yield to the Father your list of details awaiting clarity. Ask Him to answer in His timing and to give you the measure of faith required to move forward despite not knowing.

# MAKING GOOD OR MAKING AMENDS

*"You do not delight in sacrifice, otherwise I would give it; You are not pleased with burnt offering. The sacrifices of God are a broken spirit; a broken and a contrite heart, O God, You will not despise." Psalm 51:16-17*

"Act first and apologize later." That's a motto I've heard some people live by. They believe getting their actions approved ahead of time is overrated. They don't ask permission before doing something for fear that they might be told not to do it. So, to get and do what they want, they just move forward and hope for the best. In the end, if they find they have done something wrong, then they just spend time apologizing and making amends.

Jonah may have liked this motto.

God commanded the fish to deposit Jonah back, probably at the crossroads of decision, Joppa. There he stood, dripping wet and no doubt a bit disoriented. God gave him new directives that mirrored the ones He had given before—"Go to Nineveh." While this might have seemed the obvious instructions He'd pass on to the newly submitted prophet, it's of interest to me that God didn't choose another fitting alternative.

**What had Jonah offered to do should the Lord allow him the opportunity (pp. 73,76)? Why do you think God didn't agree to Jonah's idea? Respond in the margin.**

*Give a Sacrifice • Jonah's obedience was more important*

The sacrifices and vows Jonah offered to make in Jerusalem were not merely thanksgiving but a visible demonstration of his atonement for his rebellion. These sacrifices and ceremonies were a mandated necessity for God's people to remain in fellowship with Him. Yet when the prophet was freed from the belly of the fish, Yahweh told him to go to Nineveh first.

Jonah's narrative ends before we discover if or when he went to Jerusalem, but we are certain that he didn't go before obeying the original command. Making good by going to Nineveh was more important than making amends by going to Jerusalem. Remember, Jonah had already made amends in his heart. The Lord knew this, and for Jonah, that was enough.

Which option do you think was more important for
Jonah to accomplish first, to go to ...
○ Jerusalem to make a sacrifice
✕ Nineveh to complete his mission

In the margin explain why you chose that option.

*Obedience should be the priority*

When we have come out of a season of disobedience and have repented
and turned back to God, it can be tempting to try to make reparations
for our actions. In a strange way we sometimes feel like we need to "be
good" to compensate for lost time. But I believe God would rather us get
right with Him, like Jonah in chapter 2, and then focus on obedience
rather than use our energy to first try to make amends to Him for our
past disobedience.

**Have you ever sought to compensate for rebellion?
What did this look like in your life?**

*Try not to repeat the same action again*

## OBEDIENCE IS BETTER THAN SACRIFICE

Another compelling illustration of this concept appears in 1 Samuel.
The prophet told King Saul the Lord wanted him to lead the children of
Israel out against the Amalekites. Samuel told Saul in no uncertain terms
to completely annihilate this enemy who had plagued God's people for
centuries. God required the death of the king, every person, and even all
the animals. They were to destroy everything and retain no plunder for
themselves (1 Sam. 15:3). Saul obediently gathered up an army of 210,000
warriors and headed out to destroy the Amalekites.

**Read 1 Samuel 15:9 in the margin. How were Saul's
actions in battle inconsistent with God's directions?**

*He did not destroy everything as instructed*

Like Jonah, Saul chose his own path instead of yielding completely to
the one mapped out by God. The Lord knew what Saul had done and told
Samuel he regretted making Saul king of the people. When Samuel went to
confront him, Saul made no attempt to hide the fact that Israel had taken
the best their enemies had to offer. Rather, he gave a compelling and stirring excuse to justify his disobedience. According to 1 Samuel 15:15, Saul

*"Saul and the people
spared Agag and
the best of the sheep,
the oxen, the fatlings,
the lambs, and all
that was good, and
were not will-
ing to destroy them
utterly; but every-
thing despised and
worthless, that they
utterly destroyed."*
**1 Samuel 15:9**

said the goods they'd taken from the land were going to be used to make sacrifices unto the Lord. Saul had foregone obedience and was looking to make amends through His sacrifice.

> In 1 Samuel 15:22, what was Samuel's response to Saul's rationalization?
>
> *obedience is better*
> *"To obey is better than sacrifice"*
>
> If you have ever prioritized making amends over obedience, what was your rationalization?
>
> *Making amends was important*

> Circle any of the following ways you've ever seen people try to make amends for disobedience. What ways would you add to this list?
> - church attendance
> - coming to the altar
> - being a "better person"
>
> - Bible study
> - ministry to the needy
> - serving in church
>
> *• Donating money to the church*
>
> In the margin record any of these or other ways you've tried to make amends for disobedience.

While Yahweh allowed sacrifices to serve as the atonement for sin, they were not His ultimate desire. God longed for people who had a heart to obey Him and remain in fellowship with Him more than He wanted a people who would choose their own path and then run to the tabernacle to gain forgiveness for their actions. Do you see that offering sacrifices was easier for King Saul than willing obedience? To obey, he had to deny his own desires and yield to God. Denying the flesh always requires effort.

Likewise, for us it is far easier to repent later than to initially submit. Obedience necessitates self-denial. Subjecting our will to the Lord's is often more difficult than kneeling at an altar and asking for His mercy. He is willing to extend mercy, but His heart is gladdened and His name glorified when His people desire to obey Him in the first place.

> In the following passage from Isaiah underline the portions that point out what Yahweh no longer desires. Circle the portions that reveal what He does desire.

"Bring your worthless offerings no longer, incense is an abomination to Me. New moon and sabbath, the calling of assemblies—I cannot endure iniquity and the solemn assembly. I hate your new moon festivals and your appointed feasts, they have become a burden to Me; I am weary of bearing them. So when you spread out your hands in prayer, I will hide My eyes from you; Yes, even though you multiply prayers, I will not listen. Your hands are covered with blood. Wash yourselves, make yourselves clean; remove the evil of your deeds from My sight. Cease to do evil." Isaiah 1:13-16

You'll notice I've highlighted one line in the passage. Please write that line exactly as it appears, and read it carefully and meditatively.

*I cannot endure iniquity and the solemn assembly*

What was Isaiah accusing the people of doing?

*Gathering to sacrifice & ask for atonement for sins*

In any way right now are you seeking to excuse, hide, or replace disobedience with "solemn assembly"?

*I don't think I am*

## ENOUGH GRACE

Hear me clearly: The Lord is always willing to forgive. He is quick to extend mercy. If you stand in need of His forgiveness today, then know that He is waiting to forgive you. Yet He desires that the knowledge of His long-suffering way and His willingness to show grace not dissuade you from the higher calling of obedience.

Speaking of His boundless grace, the apostle Paul wrote: "What shall we say then? Are we to continue in sin that grace may increase? May it never be!" (Rom. 6:1-2). Knowing the endless kindness of our God should not only catapult us to our knees to experience it but to our feet, to walk out a lifestyle of obedience that prioritizes submission to His will over all else.

What has God asked you to do?

To what divine intervention has He asked you to yield?

Get to it.

Nineveh's waiting.

**Note this week's navigation tools.**

**Day 1** *Thank God for second chances!*

**Day 2** *He delights in giving us second chances*

**Day 3** *No shortcuts with God*

**Day 4** *Move forward step by step in faith*

**Day 5** *Obedience is better than sacrifice*

# Session 5
## VIEWER GUIDE

*"So Jonah arose and went to Nineveh according to the word of the LORD. Now Nineveh was an exceedingly great city, a three days' walk. Then Jonah began to go through the city one day's walk; and he cried out and said, 'Yet forty days and Nineveh will be overthrown' " (Jonah 3:3-4).*

You get an exceedingly ~~great~~ ~~opportunity~~. (to see God move in supernatural ways)

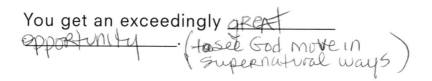 God can make the impossible possible.

Sometimes your greatest message is the mess of your life.
- Don't try to hide what God has done in your life.
- Your mess becomes your message.

God can <u>Redeem</u> the parts of your life you thought were <u>Wasted</u>.

You get divine _Anointing_.

> When we are obedient to God and His anointing is on it, we can expect huge things.

*God's anointing on small obedience can have huge Ripple effects*

> The Holy Spirit must mark us so that others know we serve a different God.

> Simple _obedience_ stamped with God's _Anointing_ will do far more than you can imagine.

You get supernatural _Results_.

> When we come face to face with God and respond in obedience, we will see supernatural results.

# INTO ALL THE WORLD

# A GREAT COMMISSION

*"So Jonah arose and went to Nineveh according*
*to the word of the LORD." Jonah 3:3*

This past Sunday I went to visit a wonderful church in the Dallas area. I'd heard so much about it and finally had an opportunity to attend. I walked my boys over to Sunday School, then parked myself up in the top row of the balcony. I was enthralled by the worship experience and was captivated by the pastor's message.

That particular Sunday marked their 10th anniversary, and the pastor shared a reminder of the core values of the church. His message boiled down to one simple church objective. He said: "We are here to make disciples, to call people to be fully devoted followers of Jesus Christ."

As is my church's tradition, I almost waved my hand in the air and shouted "Amen." Fortunately, I caught myself just in time to remember that I was in a more subdued crowd and might get thrown out by the ushers.

So I just sat and admired this pastor and church's simple aim that he stated emphatically would never change. He proclaimed their church's mission with authority because they didn't come up with it; Jesus did.

**Underline the three English action verbs in Matthew 28:19.**

"Go therefore and make disciples of all the nations,
   baptizing them in the name of the Father and the Son
   and the Holy Spirit" (Matt. 28:19).

While I hope you've been contemplating your personal divine interruption in light of Jonah's experience, we obviously can't ignore the specific call God gave in this book and to this prophet. While the details of Jonah's message to the Ninevites differed from Matthew 28:19, the purpose of God is clearly the same. God said go to those who do not know Him and extend His mercy. This theme directly connects our study of Jonah to the New Testament principle of evangelism.

God's heart is set on seeking out and reaching those who would otherwise be positioned to receive divine judgment. The Book of Jonah taught ancient Israel and teaches us today the priority God has always placed on reaching the lost with the opportunity to receive His compassion.

This primary theme of Jonah mirrors the heart of God and shines a spotlight all the way to Jesus' time. God gave the Old Testament prophet a command that parallels the New Testament Great Commission.

**How do God's instructions to Jonah (1:2) differ from the message Jesus gave the disciples (Matt. 28:19)?**

*- Jonah was told to preach against the Ninevites*
*- Matt 28:19 says go & make disciples*

**In what ways are they the same? Prepare to discuss this with your group.**

*Both say to go out amongst the people who need the Lord*

**How do you think God's emphasis on going into the world differs from the priorities of the church today?**

*Some churches are more concerned with themselves*

As I contemplated the beauty of second chances last week, I was humbled. God's Spirit brought to mind many missed opportunities when I've had a chance to share the Lord and didn't. The times I chose to sleep on the airplane instead of engaging the person next to me who seemed hungry for conversation. The occasion I didn't turn the discussion to spiritual things because I was too embarrassed. Or, most memorably, the time I kept putting off talking to my neighbor about her salvation only to hear an ambulance racing into our neighborhood to come to her aid.

They were too late.

And so was I.

**Recall one missed opportunity to share the Lord with someone you now wish you could get back.**

## MAKING DISCIPLES AS WE GO

Jesus gave the Great Commission, as Matthew 28:19 is commonly known, at a mountain meeting with His disciples. Those words have been the marching orders for believers ever since. The first memorable word in the verse is *go*. In the Greek language *go* is an aorist participle, which means it takes on the mood of the command—making disciples. It could more accurately be translated *going*. In other words, the command to make disciples should be accomplished while believers are going about their business. "As you are going make disciples in all the nations baptizing them in the name of the Father, the Son and Holy Spirit."

While nothing is wrong with evangelism efforts specifically organized for a particular outreach opportunity, we must remember that sharing Jesus is supposed to be a way we live, not just something we do.

**Consider Matthew 28:19 in light of the normal activities of your day and fill in the blanks accordingly.**

Today, as I am going about ___getting the___,

___furnace checked___, ___looking for___,

___work___, I must also be making disciples.

**In the margin make some notes on how you can consciously turn one of the activities you listed above into an opportunity to make disciples.**

I've asked you collectively to consider a person or group you might reach out to. I hope you've put plans into place to reach someone and that you're already engaged in the process. While what you do as a group will be truly significant, what you do as an individual long after this Bible study is over will have incredibly significant residual effects.

What a powerful impact we can make if we purpose to go about the regular duties of our day with an underlying mission to make disciples—devoted followers of Jesus Christ. This way, reaching the lost won't just be relegated to the evangelism department at our church or the outreach program scheduled for the end of the month. It will be a mission on the heart of every believer, from every church, and in every city.

> Evangelism is not something to do; it is a way to live.

## YESTERDAY, TODAY, AND FOREVER

Yahweh's heart to reach the unreached has never changed. We see it in the 8th Century B.C. in Jonah's book all the way to this present age. It appears as a theme that resonates passionately in the heart of God.

Unfortunately, in our day a growing philosophy called *process theology* leads many to turn from God's passion. Listen to R. T. Kendall describe this viewpoint. He says it is the idea that: "God grows, that God is enriched by His creation, that God learns from us, that God has made us cocreators with

Him. This philosophy claims that God speaks in different ways at different times, even if it comes to repudiating what He may have done once before. ... The idea then is that God is not interested in the same things He was interested in at previous time."[1] The implication of this popular ideology is that what was once important to God may no loner be as important to Him today. Many Christians think we have the freedom to revamp biblical priorities based on the evolution of concerns in our present age.

While reading a statement like this might cause us initially to shake our heads in disgust, we'd be hard pressed to find many Christians or churches who have not succumbed to this way of thinking and living at some point. For example, it can be easy when we see the change in our culture to adapt and sculpt our values and decisions to keep up with the ever varying tide of the times. As we watch the widening gap between basic Christian principles and socially correct viewpoints, we wonder if we should "fudge a bit" to be more sensitive to the times we are living in. Or maybe we have simply begun to prioritize things that are not a priority to God. Like Jonah, we have a list of important tasks that override God's purposes for us and keep us from fulfilling His main calling. The result? Many Christians and churches have deserted the mission God gave His people for every age and every place: Go and make disciples.

> **Reread Kendall's explanation of "process theology." How have you seen the effects of this kind of thinking evident in your sphere of influence lately?**
>
> *In our lives & in society in general, we tell ourselves that what applied in Biblical times doesn't apply now.*

Undoubtedly, for many believers, reaching others is not their main concern. Yet when Jesus hung on the cross and when He gathered His disciples in Matthew 28:19, evangelism was His.

As we venture into pagan territory with Jonah over the next two weeks of study, please don't just read his story. The call is clear. It came to Jonah, and it has come to us. Get going and make disciples.

As your group or you individually work to form relationships with others in an effort to share Christ, I'd love to hear how the Lord is working. As I write, I am praying that you will see great miracles in the lives of others and in your own life as you serve. Please go to *www.goingbeyond.com* and keep me posted. I'd be honored to hear what God is doing.

Day 2

# AN EXCEEDINGLY
# GREAT OPPORTUNITY

*"Now Nineveh was an exceedingly great*
*city, a three days' walk." Jonah 3:3*

I met Manette when she was 9 years old. I was on a mission trip in Haiti and as a 17-year-old American teenager, I was overwhelmed by the living conditions young people like Manette had to endure. I questioned whether anything I could offer could make any real difference. Yet my heart was drawn to this sweet little girl because, despite a deplorable living situation, she had the brightest of eyes and an endearing smile.

On January 12, 2010, I was sitting in my house writing this study on Jonah when I got word that a horrific earthquake had ripped through the Haitian capital of Port-au-Prince. Schools, homes, and businesses had smashed to the ground, killing and wounding thousands. My heart dropped into my stomach. Manette had e-mailed me several days earlier about her excitement regarding her first year in nursing school in Port-au-Prince.

I sent e-mails and made phone calls. I desperately longed to know if anyone from the mission's organization I partner with in Haiti had heard from my sweet friend. It would be three long, agonizing days before I received a response. When I did, I discovered that Manette's school had collapsed. Miraculously, she'd escaped with only a few scratches. Not only was she fine but she was now in nearby Pignon serving and sharing Christ with others who'd fled there for safety.

Sweet relief swept over me like a cool, refreshing river. I thanked the Lord not merely for her safety and for the relationship He'd given us for the past two decades but also for her desire to share the love of the Lord with others in the midst of tragedy.

Those many years ago, I didn't think anything I could do for this girl and her third world country could have any lasting effect. It all seemed too big and devastating for one person's efforts to make any significant mark. But now I am so glad I didn't let my insecurity stop me from doing my part. I know for sure that every dollar I sent, every prayer I offered, every care package I mailed has been worth it because a girl who grew up to become a young woman is serving the Lord and serving others.

Research Jonah 3:3 in several different translations. See if you can find at least two different ways Nineveh is described. List them in the margin.

God called Jonah to walk into an overwhelming problem. Nineveh was "the biggest, strongest and wealthiest city of its day."[2] It was known not only for its size and population of "nearly 600,000 inhabitants"[3] but also its importance. It was extremely evil and corrupt. As we've previously seen, it was a nation so filled with brutality and violence that outsiders avoided it. Going to Nineveh seemed to Jonah to be an overwhelming task not merely because of its magnitude but because of the evil that prevailed in the culture. I wonder if he felt a bit like I did when considering all the work that needed to be done. Could one man with one divine mission really make an impact that would count?

Missionary Assignment

If your group has chosen Ninevites to whom you are reaching out, what seems overwhelming or impossible about working with them? Plan to discuss this in your group this week.

Consider your personal divine interruption. Make a list of what God is asking of you that seems too big or overwhelming for you to handle.

*Being able to stay in my current home seems impossible now, with no good job prospects*

## OUTMATCHED

I very frequently feel as if God has put me in a position that is beyond my ability. In fact, this seems to be my track record with God. Each time I left the hospital with a new son, I looked in shock at the nurses when they told me it was time to go home. I couldn't believe they were going to send me home with a real live baby and no handbook. When asked to share a platform with seasoned speakers and teachers I greatly admire, I often wonder how I, as a young woman, will be suited for the task. And every time I put pen to paper to write a study on God's Word, I'm just certain I won't have anything noteworthy to record.

I've become used to God's allowing me to be outmatched. It seems that this is His way: putting regular people in circumstances that are beyond their own capabilities.

**Does God seem to make a point of putting you into situations that seem too big for you to handle? If so, list some of them in the margin.**

*Blue belt test, finances*

**Choose two of the following examples of God giving what seemed to be unrealistic assignments. Answer the questions that follow the examples:**

1. Jeremiah's call and commission—Jeremiah 1:4-19
2. David and Goliath—1 Samuel 17:20-51
3. Elijah and the prophets of Baal—1 Kings 18:17-40

**How were they outmatched?**

*Jeremiah ① He felt he was too young to be a prophet*
*David ② He was only a young shepherd boy against Goliath*

**How did they feel about the situation?**

*overwhelmed, frightened*

**How did God equip them to handle the circumstances?**

*He gave them the ability & strength to do His will*

The apostle Paul knew a thing or two about feeling outmatched. While we don't know the specifics of the circumstances he faced, clearly he faced something he would have rather been without.

While Paul had been privileged to receive visions and special revelations from God and have profound spiritual understanding and wisdom, he longed to be freed from an ailment God allowed and over which Paul had no control. Clearly, he had been handpicked by God. You would think someone with so much gifting and favor would feel well-equipped to handle any situation that God would allow. Yet in Paul's situation that was far from the case.

**What did Paul call his ailment (2 Cor. 12:7)?**

*a thorn in his flesh*

Scholars have given many explanations as to what Paul's problem might have been. And while the specifics may never be known for certain, one thing is sure. Paul knew why God had allowed it.

Reread 2 Corinthians 12:7. Why did Paul say the "thorn" had been given to him? *To keep him humble*

God purposefully put Paul in a situation beyond his control. He gave the apostle a constant reminder of his need to rely on and connect with Him. Without this thorn, Paul might have slipped into arrogance, but this pressing need continually reminded him of his frailty.

You previously listed things that seem too big for you to handle right now. Choose two of them. For each one prayorfully record how those things keep you humble and more aware of your need for God.

| My Thorn | How It Humbles Me |
| --- | --- |
| *My financial problems* | *I have to trust & depend on God to deal with it* |

God could have removed Paul's ailment. He could have lightened the load. I'm sure the apostle thought that any of the three times he'd asked God to bring relief would have been a good time (2 Cor. 12:8). Indeed, He could have chosen to put Paul in a path devoid of mountains that needed moving or problems that needed solving. God could have made sure nothing would have caused the apostle to feel overwhelmed.

God could have done those things, but doing so would have annulled one of His primary purposes for His people: to teach them to tap into divine power to accomplish divine purposes.

How have you seen evidence of God's power when you were in a position that exposed your weakness?

*My blue belt test — Could not have passed that in my own abilities*

## GRACE FOR GROWN-UPS

Instead of grumbling over the insurmountable odds, this time Jonah just moved forward in immediate obedience to God's commission. He "began to go through the city one day's walk and he cried out" the message that the Lord had given him to declare to the lost pagans (Jonah 3:4).

Paul, still dealing with the thorn as a constant source of stress, taught, wrote, and ministered to those the Lord put in his path. Both Paul and Jonah had to rely on God. In spite of the odds, both men made huge impacts that affected thousands. Both learned that: "My grace is sufficient for you, for power is perfected in weakness" (2 Cor. 12:9).

Second Corinthians 12 gives us a glimpse of God's sustaining grace. While we celebrate His saving grace, never forget that more grace sustains you when you are weak. Friend, God's sustaining grace is sufficient to meet your need. You can say with Paul, "My God will supply all your needs according to His riches in glory in Christ Jesus" (Phil. 4:19).

Yes, God can meet that need that looms before you like a mountainous display of impossibility whether it's a personal insecurity or ailment that always seems to hold you back or, like me, a call to send aid into another part of the world. Your Father has enough grace to sustain, keep, and use you.

Grace for grown-ups. It's the kind of grace you need, and it's the kind that God offers. Don't waste time trying to get rid of your weakness, using it as an excuse, or explaining it away. Instead, let's take a cue from Jonah and move forward with confidence into our Ninevehs. And let's follow the lead of Paul and boast in our weakness so that the power of Christ may be reflected in it and through it (see 2 Cor. 12:9).

> End today's lesson by reading 2 Corinthians 12:9 slowly. Ask the Lord to reveal to you what weaknesses He has allowed you to experience or what "exceedingly great" problem He's let you face for the purpose of showing you and others His divine power operating through you. List them below and spend time thanking God for the opportunity to see His power in and through your life.

# SET UP TO WIN

*"Then the people of Nineveh believed in God; and they called a fast and put on sackcloth from the greatest to the least of them." Jonah 3:5*

For Christmas the boys got a machine that catapults baseballs into the air. One after the other, a motor shoots them out of a tube. When my husband first put it together, one son saw the frequency and velocity of the balls and resigned himself to defeat.

"I'll never be able to hit those balls."

He whined and complained that he couldn't experience any victory with the new game while we tried to convince him to at least give it a whirl. Finally, he stood several yards in front of the machine with bat in hand anxiously awaiting the first pitch.

I felt bad for him. He looked so worried, so apprehensive, so unsure. If only he knew what I did. The game had some gears that could easily be changed to control the speed and timing of each pitch. His father had already tinkered with them, preparing them to match the ability of our son.

He had nothing to worry about. He'd been set up to win. He simply needed to step up to the plate and play the game.

*"Jonah set out on the first day of his walk in the city and proclaimed, 'In 40 days Nineveh will be overthrown!' The men of Nineveh believed in God. They proclaimed a fast and dressed in sackcloth—from the greatest of them to the least."*
**Jonah 3:4-5, HCSB**

**According to Jonah 3:4-5, how long did Jonah's message take to begin to affect the Ninevites?**
- ○ three days
- ● one day
- ○ one week
- ○ one hour

I'm stunned when I consider how quickly the effects of Jonah's obedience began to take place. I can only imagine that Jonah must have been too. Yet after only one day on the job, conviction spread like wildfire among the people and they began to turn from their wickedness. I've never heard of anything like this before. In fact, many historians cite what happened in Nineveh as the greatest revival in human history. How could this be?

**What message did Jonah give to the people (v. 4)?**

In 40 days Nineveh will be overthrown

Nothing seemed particularly stirring about Jonah's message to Nineveh. Except for the fact that God Himself had given it, no other hugely noteworthy aspects would justify the response of the Ninevites.

The Scripture doesn't say why the people responded so quickly, but a look at history may give us some insight. In 765 B.C. and again in 759 B.C. two plagues ravaged the people of Nineveh. Disease and sickness swept across the city and its inhabitants, killing many. While they were well-sheltered from military threats by the massive inner and outer walls that surrounded their city, these plagues reminded them that they were not impervious to disaster. "These plagues, coupled with a total eclipse of the sun on June 15, 763 B.C. were enough to soften the Ninevites to Jonah's preaching."[4]

Would the arrogant and proud Ninevites have responded to Jonah had he come before the events occurred? We don't know, but recent events had no doubt sparked fears and humbled them, so they responded quickly when he came. His message met with a prepared climate and prepared hearts that had already been massaged by natural circumstances controlled by God. He'd gone before Jonah and tinkered with the gears to make sure that when Jonah stepped up to the plate, maximum results would be achieved. Jonah had been set up to win.

## THE GOD WHO GOES BEFORE

In 2 Chronicles 20 a stirring account tells of the Moabites, Ammonites, and Meunites launching an attack against Jehoshaphat, the king of Israel. With such fierce competitors, the king was afraid and sought God for help. God offered Him specific instructions and gave him specific guarantees.

*"The LORD is the one who goes ahead of you; He will be with you. He will not fail you or forsake you. Do not fear or be dismayed."*
**Deuteronomy 31:8**

Read 2 Chronicles 20:6-24, and answer true or false:

T /(F) Jehoshaphat believed Israel had enough power to overcome their enemies (v. 12).

T /(F) God said to gather their artillery for battle (v. 15).

(T)/ F Their main strategy would be to stand and see God's salvation (v. 17).

(T)/ F Praise and worship was one of their primary weapons (vv. 21-22).

T /(F) Judah set ambushes for Ammon and Moab (v. 22).

(T)/ F Ammon and Moab became distracted by Seir and began to battle against them (v. 23).

T /(F) Judah still had a lot of war to wage when they arrived to the wilderness (v. 24).

**If you had been in Jehoshaphat's predicament, how would you have advised the people to deal with the situation?**

*The same way Jehoshaphat did.*

If Jehoshaphat hadn't been fully yielded to God, being obedient and trusting His method would have been difficult, especially with circumstances so out of control and no clear strategy in place. Yet God planned to do an incredible miracle for His people that they simply had to believe to experience. He'd paved a pathway to victory on which they simply had to walk in obedience.

The result of God's work and the people's willingness to partner with Him was not only a victory in battle but an overflowing host of goods and treasures recovered from the enemy's camp. What a sweet victory.

When I was 14, I took sign language classes with my aunt. Once a week we would go to a local Christian bookstore and sit under the tutelage of a spunky young woman who was adept in the art of signing. I relished each lesson. I clearly remember her not only teaching us the signs but also having interesting discussion on the beauty and power of God's Word communicated in this way.

The teacher recounted an occasion when she sat in a service where God's Spirit was moving in an incredible way. While the preacher preached a passionate message of salvation, no interpreter signed for a group of deaf visitors who had come on that occasion. She knew they were there but at the time knew very little sign language, certainly not enough to translate an entire message. Her heart hurt for those who could not internalize the powerful truths being shared.

She didn't know how to sign all that the preacher said, but she did know how to clearly sign, "Jesus died for you." Jesus. Died. For. You. So at the appropriate time she bravely stood up, walked over to where the group was sitting, looked them squarely in the eye, and signed those four simple words.

In the next few minutes, something unexplainable happened. Tears began to flow from their eyes, and they began to flood the altar without prompting. They gathered together on their knees and came to the Lord in salvation. She knew four simple signs hadn't accomplished that. The Lord had already been at work in their hearts in ways she might never know to cause her simple obedience to have a powerful effect.

Have you ever ministered in a situation where you saw unbelievable spiritual fruit? If you were able to learn about what prepared their hearts, list those elements below. Prepare to share this with your group this week.

How can the idea of God going before you change the way you feel about stepping into "exceedingly great" opportunities and challenges He has set before you?

*More confident — the way has been prepared by Him*

I am amazed to consider the work God does to prepare the way for our obedience. We cannot see the tapestry of divine activity behind the scenes. When we are up against a task that appears too grand for us to undertake, we must remember:

1. We are right. It most likely is too big for us to handle.
2. If God is calling us to it, He will equip us for it.
3. God has been at work in the situation long before we are scheduled to arrive, and He is preparing the way for our obedience to make a difference.

Rewrite these three principles in your own words using phrases that will make it more specific to you.

1. *When we think it's too big to handle alone, we are right (we need God's help)*

2. *If God calls me to do something, he will equip me for it.*

3. *God has been at work behind the scenes preparing the way (setting us up for the win), if we'll just step up to the plate & obey the call*

Spend the remainder of your time thanking the Lord for each principle you wrote above. Ask Him to bring it to your remembrance as you face challenges this week.

# WILDEST DREAMS

*"And the man of God answered, 'The LORD has much more to give you than this.'" 2 Chronicles 25:9*

During her 25 years stint as the queen of talk television, Oprah Winfrey astounded audiences with creative surprises and memorable celebrations. In 2004 she took the amazement on the road with her Wildest Dreams tour. Her show made stops around the country, visiting people who had outlandish dreams that they longed to have fulfilled. From paying off large amounts of debt to making introductions between ordinary folks and dashing superstars, the tour's efforts amazed thousands of fans. In true "Oprah" style, dreams were not just met, they were superseded.

What's your wildest dream? Now, don't just keep reading here. Take a moment and ponder my question. Think about the divine intervention the Lord has allowed—the one that's been on your mind for the past five weeks of our time together—and let your mind wander a bit. What would be the most phenomenal outcome you could imagine would happen?

**In your wildest dreams, what would God accomplish in this situation? Respond in the margin.**

*I'd win the Publisher's Clearinghouse sweepstakes so I could be financially secure & bless others*

When Jonah went reluctantly yet obediently to Nineveh, he knew that God was eager to offer mercy (4:2), yet he was probably not prepared for the response his message received. Not only did the people respond at the end of just one day but also they "called a fast and put on sackcloth from the greatest to the least of them" (3:5). The mind-blowing fruit of Jonah's obedience didn't stop there.

**From Jonah 3:6-8 make a list of other occurrences that might have surprised the reluctant prophet.**

*The King of Nineveh covered himself w/sackcloth & issued a proclamation that everyone, man & beast wear sackcloth & fast, call upon God & repent*

When Jonah chose to walk in obedience to the word of the Lord, the result was a harvest of amazing fruit he'd probably never seen coming. Not just one community in the city or even a handful of the city's important people believed in God. Every citizen of Nineveh, from the greatest to the least, immediately believed. Conviction was so complete that even the animals were made to participate in the government-mandated fast. "Even the great Apostle Paul never experienced anything comparable to what Jonah saw. Paul never saw an entire city turned to God."[5] The story of Jonah testifies to the power of our willingness to yield to divine interruptions and leads us to consider two things: the effect the Word has on unbelievers and the effect our simple obedience has in our personal circumstances.

## A SHARP SWORD

As I mentioned in your video lesson this week, Jonah's message was not filled with eloquent prose or stunning illustrative material. It was a short message containing only five Hebrew words. He hadn't constructed an outline for the points he wanted to make or spent a lot of time sprucing up the details.

Jonah took what God gave him straight into the heart of the city and declared it. It would have taken only a moment or two for him to share what God had told him to, and yet the effects of his efforts were monumental.

Short messages with huge impact are not hard to come by in the Scriptures. In *Finding God's Will for You,* author James Devine notes that Belshazzar "saw handwriting on the wall that consisted of only four words, yet the impact was clear and convincing! John the Baptist's message was short too: 'Repent, for the kingdom of heaven is at hand' (Matt 3:2). These words are nearly the same as those proclaimed by Jesus Himself in Mark 1:15."[6] This tells us that it is not necessarily *how* the words are spoken that will affect people but rather *what is* spoken that will make an imprint on the souls of mankind.

*"For the Word of God is living and active and sharper than any two-edged sword, and piercing as far as the division of soul and spirit, of both joints and marrow, and able to judge the thoughts and intentions of the heart."*
**Hebrews 4:12**

What are your apprehensions about sharing God's Word with another? Mark any of the following that apply. I feel like I am:

- ☒ not equipped
- ☒ not knowledgeable enough
- ☒ not eloquent enough
- ☒ not prepared
- ○ not willing
- ☒ not sure (how to speak w/o coming across as pushy)

Jonah may have felt some of these things as well. In fact, we'll see in the final chapter of this book that his heart wasn't even in line with the message that gave the Ninevites opportunity to receive God's mercy. He still didn't want Nineveh to be preserved, yet God still used His Word to reap an unprecedented harvest. If you feel unsure about reaching out to the lost for any reason, join the crowd. I'll admit some people's ability to easily and seamlessly reach others is uncanny, yet my insecurities don't absolve me of responsibility. You and I can rest, knowing that while we may feel powerless, His Word is powerful. It carries the weight needed to convict sinners, draw the lost, and call all men unto Himself. We must depend on it and not ourselves to garner a response from others. Our message doesn't have to be long or profound or wonderfully crafted, just simple and significant and filled with Scripture!

**Do you know at least three Scriptures you can use at a moment's notice to minister to someone? Put their references below. If you don't know any, look up three of the ones I've listed in the margin and summarize them.**

John 3:16

For God so loved the world ...

Romans 3:23

All have sinned & full short of the Glory of God

Romans 6:23

The wages of sin is death, the gift of God is Eternal life in Christ Jesus our Lord

Romans 5:8

God demonstrates his love for us: while we were still sinners, Christ died for us

Romans 10:9

If you confess w/ your mouth "Jesus is Lord" & believe in your heart that God raised him from the dead, you will be saved.

Romans 10:1

My heart's prayer & desire to God for the Israelites is that they may be saved

Ephesians 2:4-6

Because of his love for us, God who is merciful, made us alive in Christ even when we were dead in transgression By grace you have been saved

Ephesians 2:8-9

It is by grace you have been saved - through faith - it is the gift of God, not by works

1 John 5:11-12

God has given us eternal life & This life is in his Son. He who has the Son has life, he who does not have the Son of God does not have life

## A SIMPLE OBEDIENCE

A creek runs behind our house. We can see only a small portion of this long stream that spans many miles and different properties. I was very intrigued on one occasion when someone decided to drain an overflowing pond in the area by pumping the water into the creek. The small, steady stream turned into a rushing river.

As I drove along, I noted how the quickened flow affected every other part of the watercourse. The water went over hills, down paths, under the roads, behind houses, and from property to property. The part of the creek behind my house became vastly different. It looked like a diving pool. It was beautiful. All of those homes, properties, and families were affected by one little change so many miles upstream.

I stand amazed at how one action can have a tremendous effect. Often in Scripture, one regular person followed through on one regular act of obedience, and many experienced a ripple effect. Think about the woman in 1 Kings 17. She'd lost her husband; they had little to eat and certainly nothing to spare. Yet at Elijah's bidding she took the last she had and made him some food. That one act resulted in a never-ending supply of good eats for her family until the famine was over.

Esther's act of bravely going to the king to save her people resulted in the salvation of her entire race. Consider Ruth choosing to leave Moab behind to follow her mother-in-law to Bethlehem. She met Boaz and became part of the lineage of the Messiah. Joshua just walked around Jericho's walls, and they came crashing down. Peter just kept his eyes on Jesus and was able to walk on water. Each of these scenarios provides a gripping reminder of the impact choices we make can have, even when they seem inconsequential.

**Has your life been hugely impacted by people who were willing to be obedient in a small way? Write their names in the margin, and try to contact them this week to thank them for what they did. Remember some of those details to share with your group this week.**

*Grandma*

The results of your simple obedience will be felt by those around you. So much hinges on our decision to go with God and "lean not to [our] own understanding"(Prov. 3:5). God is sitting on the edge of His seat ready to do more than you can ask or think (Eph. 3:20) if and when we are willing to submit to Him and move forward. What He has asked of you may seem insignificant, but it is not. The pumping of one pond upstream can have a trickle-down effect felt in places you can't even see.

**Are you tempted to believe that what God is requiring of you will make no difference? ☒ yes ⃝ no  Please share.**

*—Sometimes I think whatever good I do has no lasting impact*

Your obedience matters. The apology given to your spouse could galvanize your entire marriage. The small financial gift you sent to that ministry could keep their doors open. The phone call to the estranged friend could salvage a friendship. And while these results are nice, our God is more than just a dream giver. He is a wildest dreams catcher. He can do beyond that which you can imagine as He uses your obedience as a foundation for what He is building.

**Conclude today's lesson by considering this and recording your thoughts in the margin.**

The Day of Atonement is a holy day that continues to be significant on the modern Jewish calendar. The afternoon service is usually reserved for reading the entire Book of Jonah as an illustration of true repentance. A Gentile nation turning to God is the example held up for the Jews. The impact of Jonah's obedience wasn't just a message to ancient Israel. It still impacts Israel today.

Earlier in today's lesson you wrote down your wildest dream in your current situation. Stay busy dreaming! He's able to do what's in your dreams and so much more.

# THE REPENTING GOD

*"If that nation, concerning which I have spoken, turns from its evil, I will change my mind about the disaster that I intended to bring on it." Jeremiah 18:8*

Does God change His mind? Does God repent? Those are the questions my boys asked when I read them Jonah 3. They could not fathom someone as omniscient and powerful as the God I'd been teaching them about could make one decision and then decide to do something different.

I would have answered their question, if I'd known the answer. I had some research to do.

The idea of God switching gears is hard for us to contend with, isn't it? It appears to mean He made a mistake or chose a wrong option. We can't seem to reconcile that with God's perfection and holiness.

So how do we make sense of the final verse of Jonah 3?

*"When God saw their deeds, that they turned from their wicked way, then God relented concerning the calamity which He had declared He would bring upon them. And He did not do it."*
Jonah 3:10

### What concerns or questions does this verse bring to your mind?

*Can God call us to do something or go in the direction we think He wants and then change His mind?*

This is not the only place in Scripture about God relenting regarding a course of action. When the Book of Jonah was read to ancient Israel, it would have reminded them of similar situations. Remember Jonah didn't want to go to Nineveh in the first place primarily because he knew God was merciful and had a track record of recalling judgment when people responded obediently to His Word.

### Choose two of the following passages and in the margin write a summary statement about the circumstances surrounding the incidents involved.

*Moses asks God to remember that he swore to make Abraham Isaac & Israel's descendents numerous, & God relented & didn't destroy them for building the golden calf*

Exodus 32:13-14
Jeremiah 18:1-10
Jeremiah 26:13,19

Amos 7:1-6
Jeremiah 26:1-5

*Jeremiah was told to speak what the Lord commanded and if they repented, He would relent*

122

In the scenarios you considered, what does God's willingness reveal about His personality?

*He gives second chances*

What does it say about His intentions?

*His intentions are for our salvation & redemption*

We can't adequately describe God. We humans have to use our limited vocabulary in our attempts to understand and communicate about Him. Any terminology we use will inevitably diminish the fullness of who God is, since our language is so inadequate to the task. For instance, the Scripture says God's "hand is not so short that it cannot save; nor is His ear so dull that it cannot hear" (Isa. 59:1). God is Spirit. He made the human body but is not limited to its functions. Yet phrases like these enable us to better relate to Him. When the word *repent* is used in reference to God, it does not have the same implication as it does when man repents.

*"The Glory of Israel will not lie or change His mind; for He is not a man that He should change His mind."*
**1 Samuel 15:29**

Consider the verses in the margin. How do these Scriptures appear to contradict God's choice of actions toward Nineveh?

*They indicate that God does not change his mind*

*"The LORD has sworn and will not change His mind, 'You are a priest forever according to the order of Melchizedek."*
**Psalm 110:4**

A human being repenting normally suggests that he or she has sinned and needs to turn from wickedness. In the Hebrew "the word most frequently employed to indicate man's repentance is *shub*, meaning 'to turn' from sin to God."[7] This was the word used for what the citizens of Nineveh did.

Since we know God is free from sin, the idea of His repenting seems contradictory until we discover a different word primarily used for God's repentance. The word is *nacham* and means "to be moved to pity."[8] When Scripture speaks of God repenting, it doesn't imply that He's done something wrong or made a mistake but just that He's chosen a compassionate response as a result of another's decision. God really hadn't changed. In this case, Nineveh had. God was simply being true to His commitment to recall judgment against a nation that turned from wickedness.

Why might the statement "God responded" be more clear than "God repented"?

*Because He is responding to our change & desire to turn from evil & sin*

123

God
repenting
=
God
responding

God repenting equals God responding. God's decision not to judge Nineveh resulted from their decision to turn from their wickedness. He didn't respond because He'd made a mistake; God responded because He is always eager to extend mercy and compassion. Doing this is true to His nature and desires. He often extends a conditional judgment that allows opportunity for mercy to intervene.

## WHO KNOWS?

Jonah went into Nineveh with a clear message of judgment for the Ninevites. But it was also a message that extended hope.

**Look at Jonah's message. Circle the part that suggested judgment, and underline the portion that reveals hope:**

"Yet forty days and Nineveh will be overthrown" (3:4).

Had God been adamant about destroying the city, He wouldn't have offered a time period for repentance. He didn't want to destroy Nineveh; God wanted them to turn from wickedness and receive mercy. The king of Nineveh must have picked up on this caveat. Knowing that in a mere 40 days destruction would descend like a dark cloud on Nineveh, he wisely suggested that they fast and pray.

Two key words in the king's comments (Jonah 3:9) are important for us to consider. When prompting the people of Nineveh to turn from their wickedness and begin to fast, he made this statement:

**Fill in the blanks:**

" _Who Knows?_ , God may turn and relent and withdraw His burning anger so that we will not perish. "

Not knowing whether Jonah's message constituted a conditional pronouncement or an unconditional decree, the king didn't attempt to assume or arrogantly suggest that forgiveness would be automatic for their change in attitude and behavior.

King David offered these same sentiments as he fasted and wept for his dying child (2 Sam. 12:22). The prophet Joel offered them as he prophesied to the nation of Israel (Joel 2:14).

None of these people pretended to be able to control or manipulate God and yet they rested in the knowledge of God's merciful tendencies and hoped in Him. They believed God was powerful enough and sovereign enough to steer their circumstances however He wished.

**When you face dire circumstances, do you normally feel hopeful like David, Nineveh's king, and Joel?**
✗ yes ○ no **How does this manifest itself in your life?**

*I try to focus on God rather than the circumstances, & trust that things will work together for the best*

I'd love to be a person who has the type of hope these three had. They left room for "who knows" in their walk with the Lord. I am impressed that such high-ranking officials and prophets didn't determine that they were so knowledgeable or in tune with God that they were certain how He would act. They simply did their part and then trusted God would do His even if what He might choose would be different from what they desired.

**What was the outcome in David's situation? What did he do in response (2 Sam. 12:16-20)?**

*His child died. David washed, changed clothes & ate.*

*(because he could not change God's decision)*

Will God always call off judgment? Will He miraculously change the situation you currently face? Will that lost loved one see Him clearly and get saved? I don't know, and neither do you.

But God does, and knowing that He longs to be gracious and compassionate to us should be just what we need to have hope in seemingly hopeless situations. Keep praying, keep seeking, keep pressing in.

Why not?

Who knows what God may do?

Would you take a moment to consider your own country in light of today's study? Pray that humanity would be convicted and turn to Him. Thank the Lord for His willingness to be moved with pity, and ask Him to pour out His mercy on us and relent concerning judgment.

**Note this week's navigation tools.**

Day 1 *make disciples as we live our lives*

Day 2 *God puts us in situations where we feel outmatched so we will depend on him to help*

Day 3 *God prepares the way for us — sets us up to win if we obey*

Day 4 *Simple obedience can have a huge effect*

Day 5 *God longs to show us compassion if we repent*

# Session 6
## VIEWER GUIDE

*"But it greatly displeased Jonah and he became angry"* (Jonah 4:1).

We see Jonah throw a ~~temper~~ ~~tantrum~~ .

God decided to be God on his own terms, not on Jonah's terms.

Without even knowing it, we put God in a box .

We must always leave room for God to be God.

We have to ~~trust~~ God. We have to fully believe He is able and fully capable of being God.

God is good at His job.

*" 'For I know the plans that I have for you,' declares the LORD, 'plans for welfare and not for calamity to give you a future and a hope' "* (Jer. 29:11).

You have to have a _firm faith_ in God.

*"He prayed to the LORD and said, 'Please LORD, was not this what I said while I was still in my own country? Therefore in order to forestall this I fled to Tarshish, for I knew that You are a gracious and compassionate God, slow to anger and abundant in lovingkindness, and one who relents concerning calamity'" (Jonah 4:2).*

Are you throwing a temper tantrum because:

1. you don't think you got what you deserve?

2. someone else got what you don't think they deserve?

Your anger with God always _stems_ from a _problem_ with _pride_.
_(more concerned about ourselves)_
_(than we are w/ God being glorified)_

*"The LORD said, 'Do you have good reason to be angry?'" (Jonah 4:4).*

*"Then God said to Jonah, 'Do you have good reason to be angry about the plant?'" (Jonah 4:9).*

# THE UNMANAGEABLE GOD

Day 1

# MAKING DEALS WITH GOD

*"But it greatly displeased Jonah, and he became angry." Jonah 4:1*

What do you do when you've yielded to the divine intervention but things still have not turned out as you'd like? You followed God's path, resting in the comforting thought that at least some things might work out the way you wanted. Now, after the fact, you sit in stunned disbelief. Nothing turned out the way you'd hoped. Without verbalizing it and almost without even knowing it, you made a deal with God. You just knew He would hold up His end.

"OK, God. I'll do this if the result will be that."

Obviously you forgot to shake hands on it because God didn't keep His part of this one-sided deal. You are upset, disappointed, and angry with God.

Ever been there?

**Why do you think we make unspoken deals with God when choosing to yield to His will?**

**Think back. When was the last time you did this?**

You'd think after the triumphant happenings of chapter 3, we'd see more of the same in chapter 4. After celebrating the miraculous work God performed as a result of the prophet's obedience and Nineveh's response, the reader is perched on the edge of her seat, leaning in to hear what will most certainly be a fantastic finale to this riveting drama.

But we're dealing with Jonah here—a man who loved God but still seemed to love his own way a bit more. His response turned out to be anything but what we would expect from a man sent by God to deliver a divine message.

As a Bible teacher, when I prayerfully prepare a message, my hope is that its message will penetrate the heart of the listeners and bring about life change. I'm hopeful they will not just hear it but will respond. It seems that anyone would have these same hopes.

What two emotions does 4:1 say Jonah experienced?
- ○ happiness
- ○ joy
- ☒ displeasure
- ○ sadness
- ○ mirth
- ☒ anger

Why do you think Jonah felt this way?

*He didn't feel that the Ninevites deserved mercy*

*"When God saw their deeds, that they turned from their wicked way, then God relented concerning the calamity which He had declared He would bring upon them. And He did not do it."*

Jonah 3:10

At this point in Jonah's journey, the fact that God had changed His mind about sending judgment to Nineveh would have been unclear to the prophet. What we as readers see from 3:10, Jonah wouldn't have known. In fact, he would later go out to the edge of the city, sit under a self-made shelter, and watch to see what would happen (4:5).

Even before knowing God's decision, we find Jonah distressed and angry. Something displeased him. A compilation of things that happened in Nineveh could have pushed him over the edge. But we know one thing for sure. Jonah did not want mercy for his enemies. While he had agreed to obey the Lord, his emotions lagged behind. Jonah hoped they wouldn't respond and that they would receive divine judgment as a result.

When was the last time you obeyed God but your emotions lagged behind?

*When I accept jobs I don't really want because I need the income (I'm not sure that it was divine interruption though)*

What compelled you to obey the Lord despite the way you felt about it?

*I don't know if I was obeying God - I don't know what he wants me to do career wise*

Did you try to make an unspoken "deal" with God in exchange for your obedience?

*not consciously, but I do try to trust what I think He wants me to do*

Check any emotions you've ever felt because of an outcome the Lord allowed.
- ☒ frustration
- ☒ displeasure
- ☒ anger
- ☒ bitterness
- ☒ overwhelmed
- ☒ fear
- ○ underwhelmed

How did you handle this feeling? How did it affect your relationship with the Lord?

*I didn't understand but I still trust Him, because it turns out for my best (in hindsight)*

Chapter 3 uses the word *ra'ah* to describe both the evil Nineveh turned away from (3:8,10) and the calamity that God chose not to bring on them (v. 10). This same word is translated "displeased" in 4:1.

> **What might be the irony of the prophet indulging himself in what the Ninevites and the Lord had rejected? Prepare to discuss with your group.**
>
> *Jonah was preaching for the Ninevites to repent, yet he didn't want them to*

## DEALING WITH DISPLEASURE

Jonah was very clear on God's character. When he went to Nineveh, Jonah knew God likely would extend mercy if they repented. He didn't want to go for precisely that reason. He didn't hesitate to go to Nineveh because he *didn't* know God but because he *did*. While Jonah appreciated the character of God when expressed to him and to Israel, it displeased him to see God's mercy experienced by his enemies.

While we may be shocked by Jonah's response, often we can harbor the same feelings. When the ex who betrayed us, the friend who deceived us, the parent who abused us, or the offender who committed a crime against us receives God's forgiveness and even His favor, we can quickly fall into a pit of anger and frustration because we secretly longed for their demise.

> **Circle the adjectives Jonah used to describe God in 4:2. Which one have you seen God reflect most in your life?**
>
> *Gracious, Abundant, & most of all Relenting concerning calamity*

> **Have you ever been displeased when you saw God extend that same aspect of His character to someone you thought did not deserve it? Write this person's name in the margin. Why did you feel this way, and how did this feeling manifest itself?**
>
> *Yes, upset that someone who did me wrong seems to still prosper (not be punished) I felt it was unfair*

> **Compare Jonah's list of God's attributes from God's description of Himself to Moses in Exodus 34:6-7. What attribute is missing?**
>
> *Truth (doesn't leave guilty unpunished)*

*"He prayed to the LORD and said, 'Please LORD, was not this what I said while I was still in my own country? Therefore in order to forestall this I fled to Tarshish, for I knew that You are a gracious and compassionate God, slow to anger and abundant in lovingkindness, and one who relents concerning calamity.' "*
Jonah 4:2

**Do you think this omission may have been purposeful on Jonah's part? Why or why not?**

*Possibly — to justify his feelings*

God's too big for us to control. You can't pick and choose which of God's attributes you want to see displayed and when and where you want to experience them. You can't play games with God and expect to win.

A few days ago our five-year-old got upset with his father. They were wrestling, and evidently Jerry pinned him down in a position he'd been unable to get his little body freed from. He walked away in a huff and came into the kitchen where I was. His bottom lip was poked out, and his arms were crossed in front of his body.

"Mom, I'm not playing with Daddy anymore, and I'm not talking to him either. He's not playing fair."

I tried not to laugh out loud but found it difficult as I looked at the cute display of frustration from my son. This was very serious business to him. I put him on my knee and tried to explain to him that his father loved him and would never hurt him on purpose, but he wouldn't hear of it. He decided that he just wasn't going to talk to his father for the rest of the day.

I peered deeply into my son's eyes and told him that his father was playing fair but that he just felt outmatched. I asked him if he agreed with me that Dad was big and strong and powerful. He shook his head. Then I reminded him of all the times he'd appreciated his father's strength to fix, lift, and carry things. Then I explained that he couldn't choose to play with his father, try to control how his dad uses his power, and then get upset when he doesn't comply.

**Can you think of an attribute of God that you only appreciate in certain situations?** *His mercy*

**What does anger at God reveal about our desire to control Him?**

*We're usually angry because we couldn't control God (get the outcome we wanted).*

## ADULT TEMPER TANTRUMS

Jonah was very clear on who God was and what He was capable of doing. When it came to the Ninevites, he just didn't like it. Jonah was displeased with God because he wanted to control God. He wanted a relationship with Yahweh but only on his terms and according to his prescription. Jonah handled his frustration much the same way my five-year-old son handled his, just on a larger scale. He had an adult-sized temper tantrum.

**What do your adult-sized temper tantrums look like?**

*Feeling bitter, displeased w/the outcome It wasn't "fair"*

**Read about Jonah's temper tantrum in the margin. Turn in your Bible to 1 Kings 19:1-4 and compare and contrast it to Elijah's reaction. Be as detailed as possible.**

*He too, sat under a tree & prayed to die but he did it out of fear partly, & partly because he felt he had done what he was told & was now threatened.*

**Consider some of the events that happened before Jonah and Elijah threw their temper tantrums (see Jonah 1:17; 2:4-7,10; and 1 Kings 18:16-46). How does this make them seem even more preposterous?**

*Jonah - saved by & from whale*
*Elijah - God sent fire to burn the sacrifice after the enormity of what he did for them they still complained*

**Record three things God accomplished for you, in you, or through you last week.** *- A temp job*
*- Continued good health*
*- Courage to commit to help Eastpoint's relocation*

**How does the reality of what God is doing cause your disappointing circumstance to seem less significant?**

*It puts it into perspective*

> "But it greatly displeased Jonah and he became angry. ... 'Therefore, now, O LORD, please take my life from me, for death is better to me than life.' ... Then Jonah went out from the city and sat east of it. There he made a shelter for himself and sat under it in the shade until he could see what would happen in the city."
> Jonah 4:1,3,5

As we go into this final week of our study, consider your actions and relationship with God in light of the prophet's activities in chapter 4.
   • Are you becoming aware of a "deal" you've made with God?
   • Are you seeking/hoping to control or manipulate God in any way?
   • Are you disappointed with God about an outcome He has allowed?
Take your responses to the Lord in prayer, and ask Him to prepare your heart to hear what He wants to say to you this week.

Day 2

# GOD'S QUESTION

*"Do you have good reason to be angry?" Jonah 4:4*

*The Masoretic text is one of the oldest and most reliable Hebrew texts of the Old Testament; it is the basis of the Hebrew Bible we use today.*

Jonah 4:4 is the first time God spoke in this chapter. It's almost as if He had been waiting on the prophet to finish his tirade of whining and complaining. In fact, the Masoretic text has a *setumah* here, a grammatical device that punctuates the text with a pause when the story is read.[1] I can picture this playing out. It's like a parent listening to a whiny child and needing to take a moment before responding. After I've had my fill of the drone of one of my boys' complaining, a long pause is exactly what I need.

**Read Jonah 4:2-3 and then pause before reading verse 4. Picture Jonah as your child. What effect do you think this reading would have had on ancient readers?**

*A powerful effect — it really makes you stop and think.*

After hearing Jonah's whiny tirade, there was dead silence—a pause just long enough to wonder what happened next. The suspense continued to build and then God asked: "Do you have good reason to be angry?"

God is good at asking questions. In fact, He has a knack for asking questions for which He's already got the answer.

**Look up two of the following examples and note the questions God asked the participants.**

**Genesis 3:6-11**                         **Genesis 4:3-7**

**Genesis 4:8-10**                         **John 6:5-6** *— "Where shall we buy bread for these people to eat?"*

*- "Where is your brother Abel?" "What have you done?"*

**Why do you think He asked these questions when He already knew the answers?**

*To make Philip & Cain search their hearts & get in agreement with what they knew was true*

Divine inquiries are never for God's benefit. He knows the answer to every question. He poses questions that we may realize and agree on the truth of the answer. Answering God's questions requires a soul search that may unearth heart issues we did not formerly recognize, thereby helping us to see in ourselves what God seeks to uncover.

**What might God have been trying to uncover in the two people whose story you studied?**

*Cain – the sin of what he did in killing his brother*
*Philip – faith in God to provide food for the 5000*

The question God asked Jonah is the same the Spirit whispers to us as we teeter on the edge or fall head-long into a mound of anger. After all the moping and fury, we face this simple yet profound divine query.

*"The LORD said, 'Do you have good reason to be angry?' "*
**Jonah 4:4**

As I mentioned in our video lesson, this particular verse has made a monumental impact in my life. Not only did the Lord use it to speak to me regarding a very specific incident but He's also brought it back to my mind on several other occasions when I was leaning toward anger.

**What do you think is the importance of the question in Jonah 4:4 for anyone dealing with anger toward God?**

*It makes us stop & question whether that anger is truly justified*

Clearly, Jonah did have reason to be upset from a human perspective. Remember, the Assyrians were Israel's archenemy, and preaching to them could possibly have kept them from being destroyed if they repented. In 722 B.C., approximately "thirty-eight years after Jonah preached to Nineveh, the army of Assyria pillaged the kingdom of Northern Israel, laid siege to Samaria, and dragged every last citizen into captivity. Assyria's assimilation strategy was to intermix their conquered people in order to erase each one's former national identity."[2] They were eventually successful; at that time only the Jews in the Southern Kingdom remained unaffected by Assyria's tactics. Of course Jonah was mad. Who wouldn't be?

*"The king of Assyria brought people from Babylon, Cuthah, Avva, Hamath, and Sepharvaim and settled them in place of the Israelites in the cities of Samaria."*
**2 Kings 17:24**

**If you are disappointed or upset with God right now, in the margin list some of the logical reasons why.**

*Not so much upset as impatient – when will things come together for me?*

## OUR ANSWER

A careful consideration of God's question to Jonah and the Holy Spirit's question to us today should cause us to uncover two things: our inconsistency with God's character and our need for God's Spirit.

An accurate assessment of this question demands we consider how inconsistent our character is with God's. While we may not lack for head knowledge about God, we must translate that knowledge from our heads to our hearts. It must transform us. Jonah knew about God yet was not in any way acting like Him in this situation. This most assuredly weighed on Jonah's mind as he took God's question to the outskirts of the city (Jonah 4:5).

How do you think Jonah might have responded differently if he had had a head-heart connection?

*He wouldn't have been as upset with the mercy God showed the Ninevites*

What marks the difference between a Christian with a head knowledge of God and one whose knowledge has reached his or her heart?

*They are more aligned with God's will - not as quick to be upset or angry when trouble befalls them or things don't go their way*

I noted earlier that Jonah said God is slow to anger. This particular characteristic appears in many other places in Scripture (Ex. 34:6; Neh. 9:17; Ps. 145:8; Joel 2:13). The Book of Proverbs even elevates the trait for us to emulate (Prov. 14:29; 16:32). God is not easily angered. Aren't we glad that's the case? If He were inclined to angry outbursts, all of humanity would be suffering at every point of the day. Every form of solace demonstrates that our God has a propensity toward dispensing kindness.

Knowing that the holy, completely powerful God could be angry and yet is slow to yield to it should cause us to reconsider the anger we feel when betrayed, belittled, or just ignored. It should also cause us to question any anger we feel toward God. Knowing He could and should be angry at us and yet chooses not to be should cause us to rethink our position.

gracious

compassionate

slow to anger

abundant in steadfast love

relenting from disaster

Look at the list of God's attributes in the margin. Circle two that others are less likely to see in your life.

*Slow to anger, gracious*

In what ways do you think your life could be more effective with a greater head-heart connection?

*My connection would show up more in my outer life (appearance to others) - better balance of head knowledge about Scripture and heart to share it will allow me to share the word more effectively*

When we realize the gap between God's character and ours, the second thing that we should consider is our great need for God's assistance in molding us into His image. Since, from a human perspective, we may feel justified in our anger toward another or toward God, the only way we can ever be slow to anger is if God's Spirit is compelling us in that direction.

God gave us His Spirit for many reasons—companionship, comfort, fellowship, guidance, and counsel to name a few. But He also gave us His Spirit for empowerment. Believers should be enabled to live beyond our normal human capabilities. While we will never achieve perfection in any of

God's attributes, it can be our experience through the work of the Holy Spirit in ever-increasing measure. We can and should expect to see the fruit of God's work in our lives as He changes us daily.

**Read Galatians 5:16-23. Note the deed of the flesh from verse 20 that corresponds with our topic today.**

*fits of rage*

**What are some of the aspects of the Spirit's fruit that would annul outbursts of anger (vv. 22-23)?**

*love, peace, patience, kindness, self-control*

The fruit of God's Spirit can only be realized in the life of someone who is consistently yielding to the Spirit's work in his or her life. In other words, the inclination of our flesh will always pull in the opposite direction of what the Spirit seeks to help us do. We must totally rely on the Holy Spirit to see the effects of His work in our lives.

**How would you describe "walking by the Spirit" if you were teaching a Sunday School class?**

*Asking God's help to guide your path in your daily life*

**Consider the two attributes you circled as least likely to be seen in your life. As you've yielded to the Spirit, how have you seen evidence of God's Spirit transforming you in those areas?**

*I've tried to be more gracious & patient (slow to anger) when people anger me. (Don't always succeed, but improving bit by bit!*

**How are you participating with Him in that effort?**

*Making a conscious effort in that area & asking for His help with it*

> "If we live by the Spirit, let us also walk by the Spirit."
> **Galatians 5:25**

Divine interventions will most assuredly foster a need for divine questions. When you sense the Spirit of God asking you questions that cause you to do a bit of self-examination, be willing to agree with God about what you find hiding in your heart. He doesn't convict you to condemn you. He purposes to change you into His likeness and bring you into intimate fellowship with Himself.

End today's lesson by prayerfully considering today's divine question in light of your personal circumstances: "Do you have good reason to be angry?"

Day 3

# MISPLACED PRIORITIES

*"So the LORD God appointed a plant and it grew up over Jonah
to be a shade over his head to deliver him from his discomfort.
And Jonah was extremely happy about the plant." Jonah 4:6*

We've had a cold streak in Dallas recently. The temperature each day barely reached the high 30s, and we Texas folks aren't used to that. To make matters even more dire, our propane tank ran out of gas, leaving our house cold, the stove unusable, and hot water inaccessible. I worked on this lesson in a sweatsuit covered by a big, woolly robe. I was tucked under the covers in bed and found a bit of solace from the heat on my legs from my overworked laptop. I can't tell you how thrilled I was around 4:30 in the afternoon when a workman from the propane company came to refuel our tank. Within minutes I had my thermostat cranked up and experienced sheer joy as I began to defrost under the vent in my bedroom ceiling. Ahhh. Heat. Bliss.

Turns out, too much heat was Jonah's problem. Instead of engaging in conversation with God, he made a beeline out of town like a sullen two-year-old. He ended up at the edge of the city where he sat, watched, and hoped fire would fall from heaven to devour his enemies.

Perched there on the outskirts of Nineveh awaiting its destruction, the sun beat down on Jonah mercilessly. Sitting in a hut that probably had walls but nothing more than a leafy roof affording little protection, he must have been miserable baking under the sun's glaring rays. He'd been a basket case since he started to see revival spreading through the city he so desperately despised. His rage and passion were so infuriating that he slipped into a depression and became suicidal. This divine intervention had been too much for him to handle. Yet one simple change in temperature is about to cause a radical swing in his emotions. In a matter of moments, he went from complete despair to joyous enthusiasm.

**According to Jonah 4:6, what eased Jonah's discomfort and made him extremely happy?**
○ Nineveh was destroyed.
☒ God commissioned a plant to give him shade.
○ Someone joined him in his hut.
○ God spoke to him directly.

Why do you suppose the plant meant so much to
Jonah? Check the reasons you think contributed.
☒ the physical comfort
○ having something others didn't
☒ affirmation that God loved Jonah
○ a sense of recommissioning after all Jonah's rebellion
○ other _____

Compare and contrast Jonah's feelings about Nineveh
(4:1) with his feelings about the plant (4:6).

*displeased/angry vs happy (about the vine)*

How do his feelings about the plant clearly show a
misplacement of priorities? *He's happier to see his
own protection than he is to see God's plan done.*

If you were telling your Jonah story, what represents the
plant God has appointed in your life?

*Temp job*

In Jonah's story each of the elements in the margin
responded obediently to God's bidding. Discuss with
your group what their obedience highlights in contrast
to Jonah's lack of obedience.

wind

storm

sailors

fish

Ninevites

plant

worm

sun

scorching
east wind

While the possibility of an entire city of people being saved from peril
didn't make Jonah happy, a plant appointed by God to give him shade did.
The shade-producing plant didn't just put a smile on his face; it made him
extremely happy. He was furious about divine protection given to others
but excited and thrilled to receive a bit of his own.

Now, I admit, I'm hesitant to judge Jonah. I'm freshly aware of how
a change in temperature can put a smile back on your face. In fact, my own
giddy delight over this simple change caused me to compare it with my
concern about things far more significant.

Divine interruptions have had a way of making me more aware of
my inconsistent heart. When I'm excited by my own need being met but
not nearly as anxious to see God's purposes served, it's apparent I've got
some work to do. Divine interruptions often expose a lack of sensitivity to
His purposes and an absorption with self I was unaware existed. When the
insignificant makes our hearts race while the truly significant gets a shrug,
it's startlingly clear we've got miles between our hearts and God's.

139

As a result of your divine intervention, has God revealed to you a distance between His heart and yours? If so, describe your insight in the margin.

*— I find myself more concerned with my financial needs than His plan.*

What insignificant things have taken precedence over significant things in your life lately?

*— Worry, doubt. (instead of trusting God)*

What made this disparity clear?

## RECEIVING TO GIVE

After being overexposed to torrid weather and then delivered, you'd think God's kindness to Jonah would have softened his heart toward the Ninevites. God once again showed divine favor to Jonah, and yet Jonah was still hesitant to extend grace to others.

Are we willing to extend grace to others as God has extended it to us? Do a quick self-inventory and consider this: When God graciously takes care of our needs, shows up in our discomfort, or calms our anxieties, our first inclination should be to offer an extension of those same healing properties to someone else. His grace to us should make us more gracious to others.

*"Blessed be the God and Father of our Lord Jesus Christ, the Father of mercies and God of all comfort, who comforts us in all our affliction so that we will be able to comfort those who are in any affliction with the comfort with which we ourselves are comforted by God."*
2 Corinthians 1:3-4

Read 2 Corinthians 1:3-4 in the margin. Personalize the principle expressed in the space below. Be specific about how God has shown you comfort and how you can translate that to another.

*God has always been there (especially when I got divorced). Hopefully I can use that to comfort someone else in that situation.*

Why should those who have received an abundance of divine blessing be even more willing to give to others?

*— Out of gratitude — paying it forward*
*— To remember where those blessings come from (God)*

How do you see this notion applauded or dissuaded in our culture?

*There isn't as much attention given to those who do good*

When I was first married, an older woman shared the secret of her wonder-fully successful marriage. She said, "Every day of your lives together seek to extend as much grace to your husband as God has extended to you."

I've never forgotten that truth. Let me tell you, Jerry and I have had lots of ups and downs to navigate, but remembering this principle always brings us back to a centering point that helps us to smooth things out and move forward. Extend grace.

## A NEW ALIGNMENT

In the margin, underline the word "calamity" from 3:10 and "discomfort" in 4:6.

Interestingly, the Hebrew noun translated "calamity" in 4:2 is the same word translated "discomfort" in 4:6. On some level God allowed Jonah to experience the distress He relented in sending to Nineveh. While the humility of pagans was enough to divert the coming divine agony, Jonah's pride and self-absorption compounded his own pain.

Again we see the one in need of an alignment in this story is not just the obvious participants of chapter 3. It's Jonah whose actions needed to be shifted, and whose priorities needed to be realigned.

> "When God saw their deeds, that they turned from their wicked way, then God relented concerning the <u>calamity</u> which He had declared He would bring upon them."
> **Jonah 3:10**

> "So the LORD God appointed a plant and it grew up over Jonah to be a shade over his head to deliver him from his <u>discomfort</u>."
> **Jonah 4:6**

In what ways are the Ninevites and Jonah parallel in this narrative? In what ways are they different?

*— They were both disobedient at first, but Ninevites repented when told they were doing wrong*
*— Jonah ~~reasoned~~ obeyed with reluctance ~~doone~~ (Glad when he was helped, and did it gladly angry Ninevites recieved) (angry Ninevites recieved mercy*

Why do you think it is important for us to see our own needs in the lives of the ones we are sent to help?

*We need to remember we also need grace & compassion & mercy. If we want it, we need to show it to others*

Every now and then we need realignment, and sometimes it's our reaction to the blessing of a simple plant that makes us realize it. Like a car that is slightly off-kilter and needs to be adjusted to run smoothly, we need to park ourselves in the care of One who can regulate our thoughts, motives, and desires so that they are in sync with His.

Today consider the sensitivity of your heart toward that which God is asking you to yield. Compare the things significant to you with those significant to God. If you find any disparity, He is able and willing to soften your heart to match His desires. Ask Him to cause you to line up with His purposes—not just in action but in the deep recesses of your soul as well.

Day 4

# DIVINE OBJECT LESSONS

*"God appointed a worm when dawn came the next day and it attacked the plant and it withered." Jonah 4:7*

My niece, Kariss, is 18. My sister has done an amazing job of navigating the teenage years with her spunky and vivacious daughter. I've always had an affinity for this child. I was only 17 when she was born, and we've been told we look more like mother and daughter than aunt and niece. While she's a very good girl, a bit of disciplining is required in training even the best kid, and Kariss is no exception.

Around age 15, Kariss wasn't being consistent about keeping her room clean. No matter what tactics my sister used to encourage her to be a good steward of her space, she just wouldn't oblige. So my sister, incredible mother that she is, decided some creative correction was needed.

One day Kariss came home to find the door on her room removed from its hinges. She walked through the door frame and stood there in shock when she realized she had nothing to close. For a teenager, infatuated with privacy, this was the most horrendous discipline she could receive. When she approached her mother about the missing door, the explanation was simple.

"Kariss, this is not your house, and this is not your room. I let you live here because I love you and you are my daughter. But I can take away anything I want because I own it, and from now on I will if you don't choose to be a good steward of it."

Talk about brilliant parenting! I'd been properly schooled for the days that are soon to come when I'll have a house full of teenage young men.

Seems that my sister was not the first to pull a move like this one to teach an object lesson. In less than 24 hours God appointed a worm to attack the plant He'd provided for Jonah, causing it to wither away and die.

**What lesson might God have been trying to teach Jonah in taking away the plant He'd provided for him?**

*That He is in control*

In the margin record details of a time God took away something you enjoyed. How did you feel about His decision, and what did you learn from it?

*When I got divorced I was hurt, but in hindsight I now know it was for the best*

How does it affect the way you relate to God now? Prepare to share this with your group this week.

*It has strengthened my faith*

We don't know the type of plant God gave Jonah, but the worm probably attacked the plant at its base. Jonah may never have known why the plant dried up. From his perspective, the plant just began to wither without any noticeable explanation. It would have been hard enough to see his shade source wilting away, but not being able to figure out why or to find a solution for fixing it would have been utterly frustrating.

One of the ways we can recognize God behind events is when we can't pinpoint any other source. When things in our lives are changing—be it wilting or gaining strength—and we can spot nothing either as the culprit or as the solution to patch up the problem, we need to turn our eyes to the heavens. God's hand and purposes can often go unnoticed and unrecognized if we aren't careful to consider His participation in life's events.

*"Scarcely have they been planted, Scarcely have they been sown, Scarcely has their stock taken root in the earth, But He merely blows on them, and they wither, And the storm carries them away like stubble."*

Isaiah 40:24

Choose one of the three biblical examples in the margin. Consider the difficulty faced by the people involved and answer these questions.

What challenge did they face? — *3) cupbearers told Pharoh*
*1) — He was accused of attempted Rape — imprisoned*
*2) — He had to interpret the cupbearers dreams (also in prison)*

Why would it have been easy for these biblical characters to miss God's purposes?

*Joseph could have merely seen his awful circumstances & given up*

What lesson might God have taught them?

*Every event worked together for Joseph*

Can you see a correlation between their story and your own personal story? *mine is not nearly as dramatic*

How would knowing God is behind a life change cause you to view it and handle it differently?

*I'd be more confident about what I need to do*

## Joseph
Genesis 39:19-23; 40:1-23; 41:8-14

## Paul & Silas
Acts 16:16-40

## The Disciples
Matthew 8:23-27

## FROM BAD TO WORSE

Jonah must not have considered God behind his bad fortune, but his Heavenly Father persisted in getting His point across. Like any good parent making sure a lesson is learned in full, God continued with object lessons to make a critical point and teach an astounding life lesson. Did you note how two elements began to ravage Jonah in 4:8?

**How do you feel about the idea that God may allow hardship to relay spiritual instruction?**

*we're strengthened in hard times & can learn from it*

storm

Jonah's call to Nineveh was the overarching divine intervention in the book. Yet small interventions fill the narrative.

**In the margin note how each of the elements might be considered a divine intervention.** *God was showing Jonah He is in control & showing him what he could have done to Ninevites, but was merciful*

big fish

**How have you seen smaller interventions in your life?**

*all the time — many times I've felt God's protection over me*

Jonah was in complete despair. He used the same root word as in verse 7 for how the worm *attacked* the plant to indicate the burden of the hot sun.[3] Jonah felt he might wither under the hot sun just as the plant had because of the worm. He must have felt under a curse. Not only had he been sent on a mission he didn't want, and was disgusted at the outcome of, but now he couldn't even find a comfortable place to recuperate. He was not merely emotionally spent, he was also physically tormented. Nothing seemed to be going his way. He was so distraught that for the second time in this narrative he considered death to be a more suitable option.

withering plant

scorching sun and east wind

**Why do you think the enemy may want to disguise difficulty used by God as punishment sent by God?**

*To try to make us turn from God*

I've met many people whose stories seem to mirror Jonah's. I'm sure you have too. It just seems one difficulty after another makes its way into their lives even though they seemed to be yielded to God's divine interruptions.

First the "plant" and then the "sun"; then the "scorching wind" wreaked havoc on Jonah. It can be easy for us to question God's wisdom and love as we stand on the sidelines for someone else or as we deal with our own string of complicated circumstances.

Do you know a person whose circumstances resemble Jonah's? Write his or her name in the margin, and list some of the circumstances they face.

*Alecia – son committed suicide .. court battles w/ex*
*Francine – Illness, financial hardships,*

If you've had a string of your own difficulties, have you attributed them to God or something else? If so, what?

*Usually blame myself*

How have these instances made you feel? Have they caused you to seek God more or less? Have you remained encouraged despite the difficulty? If so, how?

*I seek God more & try to have faith that He will always take care of me.*

Don't miss God's concern, care, and attention to detail when He crafted the specific methods to teach Jonah. The plant wasn't just any old type; it had to be substantial enough to form a roof and provide shade. While many animals could have made Jonah's stay uncomfortable, God chose a worm to harm the plant. Finally, the hot wind came in from the east. According to Jonah 4:5, the prophet had gone east of the city. This means he could not have benefited from any protection the huge walled city could have afforded him on the other side. God was strategic and detailed with the methods used to relay divine purposes to His beloved prophet.

**How might God's involvement in Jonah's circumstances encourage the person you've listed in today's lesson?**

**Carefully considering circumstances you have faced, how can you see God's careful planning?**

All hardship does not come from God, but we must consider the divine implications of our difficulties. If we only see the physical aspects, we may miss the deeper spiritual truths our Father is teaching us. God desires the same from us as from Jonah—an intimacy of relationship that molds our hearts into His image. Even if it takes a storm, a fish, a plant, a worm, and a hot east wind, He'll bend over backward to get it done.

If you face a trying circumstance, then please know you can run to a secret place (Ps. 27:5; 31:20). Like the eye of a storm, peace prevails in God's presence, even when chaos ensues all around. God has a sacred place of immunity from anything outside His will for us. He will meet you there, offering you the best of Himself and His purposes. Consider your life circumstances as divine lessons. Ask the Lord to open your eyes to see what He may be teaching you. Then open your heart to receive and retain the lessons.

# A FABULOUS ENDING

*"Should I not have compassion on Nineveh,*
*the great city?" Jonah 4:11*

I saw a movie last night with a couple of girlfriends. We made our way to the local theater, eager to see a flick we'd been awaiting. Through the entire film we sat riveted by characters and events intricately woven together. We shed a few tears, held our breath a few times, and stayed completely enthralled. But after two hours we felt shocked when the credits rolled. People started to leave, but none of us moved a muscle. We were stunned.

Was that it? Our jaws hung open in disbelief. We wanted questions answered, plots completed, and issues resolved. We'd been left hanging in more ways than one. The movie was great, but the ending left us disappointed. What's a movie without an ending that ties up all the loose ends?

**Open your Bible to Jonah 4:9-11 and read the passage.**
**What questions would you still like to see resolved?**

*What happened to Jonah?*

You might be unsettled as the story comes to an end. Unlike the children of Israel, who made it to the promised land, Job, whose life of misfortune ended with a tenfold return, or Joseph, the scorned brother who became a ruler, we have no idea what happened to Jonah. The screen just fades to black, and we sit pondering how his life unfolds.

While we are tempted to consider what we're not told, our time is better spent focusing on what we are. We find the ending of Jonah's story leaves us with much to celebrate, ponder, and incorporate into our own lives.

## GOD'S PERSPECTIVE

Jonah's final verses offer us a peek into the heart of God. He spoke more in this passage than He did throughout the rest of the book to share His thoughts and perspectives with the surly prophet. Whenever God's words are concentrated in a compact portion of Scripture, I sit forward to listen. For the majority of this chapter, He'd been giving Jonah an object lesson. Now God sought to be sure the point was clear.

In one sentence, summarize God's message from
each verse.

Jonah 4:9 *after the way you were shown mercy do you have any right to be angry?*

Jonah 4:10 *you care about this vine you had nothing to do with, so should I not care about a whole city of people I created?*

Jonah 4:11

Prayerfully consider the spiritual principle from each
summary you wrote. Note your insights for each verse.

Jonah 4:9 *If I've had (or want) mercy shown to me I have no right to be angry when God shows mercy to others (even if it seems they don't deserve it)*

Jonah 4:10 *I care about things instead of what's important*

Jonah 4:11 *God cares about the big picture (people, not things)*

For the second time God asked Jonah a question. The first time he refused
to answer and turned away from the conversation (4:4-5). This time Jonah
"responded sharply with what was most likely a Hebrew expletive."[4]

Jonah's anger was now directed at something different, and while
God's questions sounded similar, they were directed at different objects.
Initially, God's question focused on Nineveh. Now God's question focused on
the plant. Jonah found himself face to face with the reality of God's perspective: Jonah cared about a plant. God cared about people.

Consider your divine intervention. What has it revealed
to you about God's perspective, and what should be
important to you right now?

*What is God's plan for me*

As God's perspective has become more clear, how
have you refocused your outlook and reorganized your
activities to reflect this change?

*I'm reminded to keep things in perspective & look at what God's plan is*

In the first and final video lessons, I've told you about our sweet third son, Jude. He is now almost two years old and is a delight to our family. His entry into our lives has caused all of us to reorganize our schedules, shift our plans, and reorchestrate our habits. We have had to adjust our living space and reconsider our priorities to fully yield to this divine intervention who is an incredible gift from God.

Every time little Jude smiles at me or I cuddle with him in the wee hours of the morning when he cannot sleep, I remember that God's perspective is so much more grand than my own. It is bigger, better, and more important than the little things that cloud my judgment and seem to exhaust my resources. Whether or not Jonah ever realized this is unclear, but I want to be certain that I do. You too?

**Early in our study we renamed interruptions as divine interventions. How has Jonah's story helped you make this change? Share your reflections with your group.**

*Yes, it reminds me of the proper perspective*

This simple truth to internalize is more difficult to incorporate in our daily living. Seeing life through divine lenses affects our lives in every way. Considering things from God's vantage point gives us a filter to view the tangled web of earth's realities, thereby allowing us the divine momentum we need to move forward toward His goals in our lives.

*"Oh, the depth of the riches both of the wisdom and knowledge of God! How unsearchable are His judgments and unfathomable His ways!"*
**Romans 11:33**

**What does Romans 11:33 conclude about the wisdom and knowledge of God?**

*We can't understand His ways fully*

Maybe you need God's perspective as you face your divine intervention. Possibly you remain unclear as to what God would have you do and His perspective regarding the circumstances you currently face. Maybe you feel a bit discouraged because you wonder if you'll ever see clearly enough.

Romans 11:33 seems to suggest that knowing God's will and perspective is beyond the reach of mere humans. While His ways are unsearchable and His methods beyond our ability to comprehend, He will graciously lift blinding veils and give revelation to those who come in humility with open hearts to hear, receive, and obey His Word.

If we lean to our own understanding, logic, and wisdom, divine perspective will remain hard to come by. But to those willing to become like children and submit to an object lesson broken down into its most simple parts, God promises to reveal His will and His perspective with startling clarity.

*"At that time Jesus answered and said, 'I praise You, Father, Lord of heaven and earth, that You have hidden these things from the wise and intelligent and have revealed them to infants.'"*
Matthew 11:25

**From the following verses, record reasons why people often find it hard to gain God's perspective.**

Psalm 25:14 *We don't come to the Lord fearfully*

Proverbs 9:10 *We don't know God*

Isaiah 66:1-2 *We're not humble & contrite*

2 Chronicles 16:9 *Our hearts aren't fully committed to Him*

James 1:6-8 *We doubt + (don't trust/believe fully)*

James 4:6 *We're not humble*

James 4:8 *We don't come to God*

**Have you ever found gaining God's perspective difficult? Why do you think that might have been?**

*Yes — I don't know why. Sometimes I don't know what he wants me to do*

## IN THE END …

The beauty of the ending of this story is seeing how God went out of His way to shed light on His thoughts to a rebellious and stubborn man who was hesitant to cooperate. It's astounding that He'd take the time, energy, and effort not to just make commands but to mold a heart as well. The same care God had for Jonah is the same care He has for you.

**What does God's willingness to shape Jonah's heart reveal about His character?**

*He is merciful & cares about us & what we become*

**What does it say about God's love for Jonah?**

*He loves him enough to discipline him*

We do not know whether the prophet responded. What Jonah did next is unclear. The screen has faded to black, and yet I'm not disappointed after all because what happened with Jonah after this is not important. What's important is what will happen with you. When you read the final line, record your final thoughts, and flip this final page, the question is: How will your life unfold as a result of what you've studied?

- Will you begin to see life interruptions as divine interventions?
- Will you respond with renewed perspective when you encounter complex circumstances?
- Will you yield to God's instructions instead of seeking to run in the opposite direction?
- Will you be more willing to seek out the Ninevites and offer them the same mercy God has extended to you?

**Note this week's navigation tools.**

**Day 1** *Are we obedient because we "expect" something from God?*

**Day 2** *Do you have good reason to be angry?*

**Day 3** *God's grace should make us more merciful to others*

**Day 4** *We must consider deeper meaning of our interruption*

**Day 5** *God's ways are a mystery, but if we have a true spirit to know his will, He'll reveal it to us.*

The rest of your story is yet to be written.
The pen of heaven is waiting.
The perspective of God is offered.
Onward, modern-day Jonah.
The best is yet to come.

*— God will hear us and always answer us*

# LEADER GUIDE

In a childhood image Jonah sits in the whale at a desk with an oil lamp for light. Even swallowed up by sea life, he had not been upheaved from his normal life. It's far from accurate. Welcome to *Jonah: Navigating a Life Interrupted!* We can all agree that Jonah's life was more interrupted than this happy preschool image proclaims. Through this study, you'll guide women to see life's interruptions from God's point of view instead of their own.

The videos are available in the Leader Kit (item 005189429) as well as by download on *lifeway.com/women*. While it's possible to do the study without the videos, your group will be missing out on insights and teaching.

Weekly meetings require 60-90 minutes. Each session guide contains more questions than you'll have time to discuss. Choose those you will use.

Set up a comfortable environment for your discussion time. Snacks and drinks may be served each week. Arrange seating in a circle so all women can see each other. Much of your group time will be spent conversing about your own stories. Make sure women know that confidentiality is expected so that it will be a safe place to share their stories.

Start promptly to honor everyone's time. If your group is larger than 8-10 women, split into small groups for discussion and watch the videos together. Take note of the video times as they vary each week. Explain to your participants that you will facilitate the discussion, but you will not be lecturing. You will be learning together.

Pray for the women during your daily time with God. Pray that the members will hear God's Word and respond.

Before your first session, prepare a sign-up sheet with names, e-mail addresses, and phone numbers. If possible, have someone make copies for everyone in the group during the session. Put the list, extra pens, pencils, Bibles, and member books out before each session.

## Starting a Bible Study

1. Enlist volunteers to facilitate discussion groups if you need more than one group. Ask women to be in prayer over the study, that God will prepare the hearts of the participants and draw them to Him.
2. Secure a room or home and decide on a time for each week's study.
3. Determine if snacks will be served and who will bring them.
4. Organize childcare if needed.
5. Publicize the study in your church and community. Share about the study with your friends and neighbors; use the promotional video segment during church services or other events.
6. Supply member books for the participants to purchase at the introductory session. Make scholarships available for those who cannot pay.
7. Provide a DVD player and TV for each session.
8. This resource is available for credit from Christian Growth Study Plan. Call 1-800-968-5519 or *www.lifeway.com/CGSP*. Continuing Education Units contact information: 1-800-968-5519 or *www.lifeway.com/CEU*.

## Session One

**Before the Session**
1. Preview the video for session 1.
2. Read the Introduction (p. 5) and About the Author (p. 4). Underline a few key phrases as a reminder for step 2 of "During the Session."
3. Set out the following: cell phone, laptop, book, map, child's toy, video.

**During the Session**
1. What images come to mind when you think of Jonah? This study will urge us to take the lessons Jonah learned and apply them to our lives. Consider these objects. Do they represent a satisfying place or an interruption to you? Let the women respond as you show each item.
2. Discuss the theme of the study: Life's interruptions can be seen as divine interventions. Introduce the study using the phrases you underlined in the Introduction and About the Author.
3. Direct members to pages 6-7 for viewer guide. Show session 1 [41:46].
4. If time permits, ask what stood out in the video. What interruptions in their lives have turned out to be obvious divine interventions?
5. Explain that each week will consist of five days of homework. Encourage members to complete all the work.
6. Share prayer requests. Pray for your participants. Pray for their requests and that they will be challenged by studying Jonah.

# Session Two

**Before the Session**
1. Preview the video for session 2.
2. Most of this session will be spent sharing résumés (p. 19) and stories of divine intervention (p. 22). Prepare to share your stories first to set a pace and an example for the group. Don't force anyone to share, but gently remind participants this is a safe environment for sharing.

**During the Session**
1. As women enter, explain that tonight will be a time for sharing their résumés and stories of divine intervention from week 1, so that if they need to review their answers, they can do so.
2. God singled out and pinpointed you as His partner for a particular project (p. 17). How do you feel about being God's partner?
3. Invite everyone to share their résumé from page 19 and their story of divine intervention from page 22.
4. Start by briefly sharing your stories; guide the women in sharing their own, one at a time. Be mindful of time but try not to rush the women.
5. Now that you have shared a little bit of yourselves, pray for each other. Pair up the women. Instruct each to pray that the study of Jonah will profoundly affect her partner's life. Allow them to share prayer requests quickly with one another and pray for those as well.
6. Watch the session 2 video [47:58].
7. If time permits, discuss the video. Are they being challenged to arise and go? Are you glad God is not like you and you cannot grasp Him?
8. Close by asking for prayer requests and praying for group members.

# Session Three

**Before the Session**
1. Preview the video for session 3.
2. On a poster, write out James 1:14-15 in the New Living Translation, each step to the path of destruction on a different line. Example:
    > "Temptation comes from our own desires,
    >     which entice and drag us away.
    >     These desires give birth to sinful actions.
    >     And when sin is allowed to grow,
    >         it gives birth to death."
3. As you complete the session 2 homework, pay special attention to group discussion questions on pages 43 and 49.

**During the Session**

1. Welcome participants as they enter. Offer snacks or drinks, if available. Ask each member if she'd be willing to share her story of the downward spiral that she outlined on page 43.
2. Page 38 contains an excerpt from a devotional. What phrases did you underline? Why did those stick out to you?
3. Like Jonah, have you had a time when you didn't want to sense God's presence? How did you answer the question at the bottom of page 40?
4. Did Jonah's choice to put himself in exile, the worst thing most Israelites could imagine, hit home with you in any way? How?
5. Ask women who are willing to share their stories of downward spiral.
6. Refer to your outline of James 1:14-15. Can you see how each of these stories, including Jonah's, follows these steps? Guide the women in writing the step Jonah took that matches that section of verse (for example, Temptation comes from our own desires = Jonah thought the Ninevites didn't deserve deliverance).
7. How did the pagans urging Jonah to pray relate to the world and the modern church (p. 49)? Don't tear down the church, but consider how we can improve.
8. Discuss the first question from page 52.
9. Play the session 3 video [32:19].
10. Who do we know who needs to hear Jonah 2:9? Discuss people or a group of people to whom you need to minister—your Nineveh. Urge members to return with ideas for next week's session.

## Session Four

**Before the Session**

1. Preview the video for session 4.
2. On a poster, write the four principles for reconciling with God (p. 58).
3. Print or write out for yourself: Psalm 28:2; 63:4; 119:48; 141:2.

**During the Session**

1. Welcome participants as they enter. Offer snacks or drinks, if available.
2. Discuss how they would act after being unable to find the restaurant (p. 59). Discuss responses to the last question on page 59.
3. Refer to the first question on page 60. Make a list of the spiritual signs that can show a person is off course. Brainstorm as many as possible.

4. Ask a volunteer to read Jonah 1:8-10. Why did Jonah avoid some of the questions the sailors asked? Why would Jonah confess that he was running from the Lord?
5. Discuss responses to the question beginning "Recall a time ..." (p. 61).
6. Donna Otto said not to think that every good opportunity that came along was God's will (p. 62). Where have you seen this in your life?
7. Have you ever seen an example where a change was not permanent because someone's heart was not in it? When? (Children might be a good place to start.) Remind the women of 1 Peter 2:2, which says we have to "grow up" in our salvation.
8. Read aloud John 5:39-40 from The Message. Discuss your answers to the last question on page 67.
9. Ask if anyone would be willing to share her answer to the first question on page 76. Share first to get the conversation started.
10. Play session 4 [34:33].
11. Discuss specific ways you might minister in your community. Start with places your church(es) are already working, but think beyond that. Ask women to share ideas they came up with last week.
12. Tell the women you are all going to participate in the pattern and posture of prayer; it will be up to them to supply the passion. Ask them all to close their eyes and lift their hands. Read over them the Scriptures you prepared in "Before the Session." Personalize the Scriptures for your group. Encourage the women to spend time praying the Scriptures that speak to them this week during their study.

## Session Five

**Before the Session**
1. Preview the video for session 5. As you work through the week's study, pay special attention to the group discussion question on page 89.
2. Touch base with participants this week through e-mail or a phone call. Encourage them to keep up with their homework. Ask them to be ready to share their second-chance story they outlined on page 89.

**During the Session**
1. Welcome participants as they enter. Offer snacks or drinks, if available.
2. This week we looked at a lot of second-chance stories from the Bible. Praise God that He gives us second chances! Which story hit home with you the most? Why?
3. How did you respond to the last question on page 83?

4. What piece of jewelry do you really treasure? How would you feel if you lost that special piece? What would you do to find it? Discuss responses to the last question on page 88.
5. Discuss the first two questions on page 89. If helpful, sketch out answers and ideas on a whiteboard or poster board.
6. Share the second-chance stories you outlined (see the last paragraph on p. 89). Spend time letting each woman tell her story.
7. Ask someone to read Jonah 3:1-3 aloud from her Bible. Discuss the second question on page 95.
8. In day 4 we talked about John 16 and Jesus' words proclaiming the Holy Spirit. How did you respond to the first question on page 96?
9. Day 5 was about rebellion and making amends. Did you have a specific time of rebellion against God in mind? How did you try to "make up" for this rebellion to God?
10. Play session 5 [42:02].
11. Consider Priscilla's charge from the video to ask for guidance and supernatural power for those you need to serve. Ask someone to pray for this supernatural power as you close.

## Session Six

**Before the Session**
1. Preview the video for session 6.
2. On a whiteboard, write this paraphrase of Matthew 28:19—"As you are going, make disciples in all the nations, baptizing them in the name of the Father, the Son, and the Holy Spirit."

**During the Session**
1. Read aloud the version of Matthew 28:19. Ask members to refer to page 106 and share how they compared this verse from Matthew with Jonah 1:2. Also share answers to the third question on that page.
2. Read the quote in the margin of page 107. On the whiteboard or poster board, brainstorm places you go in a normal week where you might be able to share the gospel.
3. Has your group decided on a specific group to be your Nineveh? Work together on a plan of action, if you haven't already. Discuss responses to the missionary assignment question on page 110.
4. Ask the group to share responses from the group discussion question at the top of page 117.

5. Would you consider sharing your wildest dream (p. 118)? Start by sharing yours. It doesn't have to be super-spiritual.

6. Ask volunteers to read aloud Isaiah 55:11 and Romans 10:8. What do these verses say about the Word of God? Discuss the importance of speaking God's Word to others, especially nonbelievers.

7. Share stories from the group discussion question (top of p. 121).

8. Ask volunteers read aloud the following verses: 2 Samuel 12:22; Joel 2:14; Esther 4:14; Jonah 3:9. What is the repeated phrase in these verses? What does it suggest about God's decisions? Review day 5 if women are having trouble answering.

9. Play session 6 [36:49]. With any remaining time, discuss issues and questions that arise from the video.

10. To end your session, take prayer requests.

11. If you can, plan your end-of-study celebration for next week. The video will be short, giving you plenty of time for discussion and partying!

## Session Seven

**Before the Session**

1. Preview the video for session 7—it is a quick, seven-minute wrap-up.

2. Gather any supplies for your end-of-study celebration, if one has been planned. Compile a list of a few more studies being offered by your church or that sound interesting to you. You can browse studies at *www.lifeway.com/discipleship*

**During the Session**

1. How do you feel about ending our study? This might be a good time to inform participants of other studies being offered soon at your church, or let them pick another study they'd like to do together soon.

2. How did you respond about making deals with God (p. 129)?

3. Share responses to the group discussion question on page 131.

4. From page 136 discuss the difference between a Christian with head knowledge of God and one whose knowledge has reached her heart.

5. Amidst all his anger, a shade tree made Jonah extremely happy. He was even more angry when it was taken away. What has God taken away that made you furious? Share the stories you recorded on page 143.

6. Ask participants to recall the divine interruptions they've focused on throughout the study. How has studying Jonah helped them or forced them to see the situation in a new way?

7. Why is it hard to gain God's perspective on a situation (p. 148)? How can we urge one another to seek God's perspective and keep it as our focus?
8. Recall once again the Nineveh your group has chosen and the steps you've considered in pursuing that ministry. Make a definite plan, with a time and place, to serve and minister to this group of people.
9. Watch session 7 [7:07].
10. With remaining time, celebrate your study of Jonah. Build one another up and point out changes that have taken place during the last seven weeks. Encourage women to keep studying God's Word through group and personal Bible study.
11. Take prayer requests. Pray for the women, making sure to include Jonah 2:9 (HCSB)—"Salvation is from the LORD!"

# ENDNOTES

## SESSION 1

1. *A Walk Thru the Book of Jonah* (Grand Rapids, MI: Baker Books, 2009), 11.
2. J. Vernon McGee. *Jonah: Dead or Alive?* (Los Angeles, CA: Church of the Open Door, 1984).

## SESSION 2

1. Sarah Young. *Jesus Calling* (Nashville, TN: Thomas Nelson, Inc., 2004), 247.
2. Hal Seed. *Jonah: Responding to God in All the Right Ways* (Dayton, OH: New Song Press, 2008), 31-32.
3. John Walton. *Jonah: Bible Study Commentary* (Grand Rapids, MI: The Zondervan Corporation, 1982), 14.
4. Seed, 33.
5. Walton, 17.

## SESSION 3

1. James Limburg. *Jonah: A Commentary* (Louisville, KY: Westminster/John Knox Press, 1993), 49.
2. *A Walk Thru the Book of Jonah*, 19.
3. R. Laird Harris, ed. *Theological Wordbook of the Old Testament*, vol. 2 (Chicago, IL: Moody Press, 1980), 557.
4. Ibid., 912.
5. Limburg, 70.
6. Ibid., 72.

## SESSION 4

1. Paul J. Achtemeier, gen. ed. *Harper's Bible Dictionary* (San Francisco, CA: Harper & Row, Publishers, 1985), 507.
2. Warren W. Wiersbe. *The Bible Exposition Commentary*, vol. 1 (Wheaton, IL: Victor Books, 1989), 234.
3. Walton, 35.

## SESSION 5

1. R. T. Kendall. *Jonah* (Tyrone, GA: Authentic Publishing, 2006), 150-151.
2. Seed, 76
3. Devine, 109.
4. Seed, 78.
5. McGee, 34.
6. Devine, 111.
7. Harris, 571.
8. Thomas Edward McComiskey. *The Minor Prophets*, vol. 2 (Grand Rapids, MI: Baker Books, 1993), 581.

## SESSION 6

1. Limburg, 93.
2. Seed, 108.
3. Devine, 149.
4. Walton, 60.

## One In a Million:
### Journey to Your Promised Land

Every woman is on a journey. Join Priscilla on an exploration of the Israelites' journey from Egypt to a land of deliverance. You'll discover that the road to your promised land may be bumpy, but it is worth every mile. In looking carefully at the two (out of two million) who crossed over the Jordan and into the Promised Land, we find direction for our own spiritual lives. *(7 sessions)*

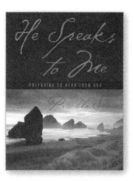

## He Speaks to Me:
### Preparing to Hear from God

Join Priscilla on an exciting adventure in discovering how God spoke to the boy Samuel, how he responded, and how God speaks to believers today. *(7 sessions)*

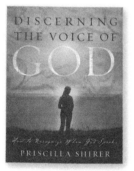

## Discerning the Voice of God:
### How to Recognize When God Speaks

Learn to recognize God's character, language, and tone of voice as you spend time in His Word and understand the role of the Holy Spirit. *(7 sessions)*

## Can We Talk?
### Soul-Stirring Conversations with God

Open the doors of communication with God through *Can We Talk?* While you will learn more about God's Word, the primary purpose of this un-Bible study is to equip you to have intimate conversations with the Creator of the universe! This unique video teaching series engages the hearts and minds of busy women through contemporary stories and a simple four-part method of dissecting the Scriptures. *(6 sessions, plus introduction)*